MIRACLES, MOONS, AND MADNESS

MIRACLES, MOONS, AND MADNESS

S.C. Ryder

ARCHWAY
PUBLISHING

Archway Publishing books may be ordered through booksellers or by contacting:

Archway Publishing
1663 Liberty Drive
Bloomington, IN 47403
www.archwaypublishing.com
1-(888)-242-5904

Cover art by Kelly Hall, Graphic Designer
inksolutions@live.ca
1-250-689-8085

ISBN: 978-1-4808-1067-9 (sc)
ISBN: 978-1-4808-1066-2 (hc)
ISBN: 978-1-4808-1068-6 (e)

Library of Congress Control Number: 2014915156

Printed in the United States of America.

Archway Publishing rev. date: 08/21/2014

For Karo, through it all, always there,

For Kim, only a phone call away,

For Kimberley, who took over the reins for my journey back.

MIRACLES, MOONS, AND MADNESS

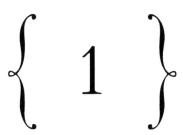

{ 1 }

NICK AND I MET IN A BAR, PROBABLY NOT THE MOST ROMANTIC OR unique setting but that was the way it happened and I fell in love just like that. I had been playing ball in a slo pitch tournament since early morning, and I was hot and sweaty and had two incredibly black eyes from being hit in the face by a rogue ball three nights earlier. He came into the bar holding a cane that helped support his limp – he later told me it was the result of a vehicle accident a year earlier. Destiny I thought! We talked for hours and drank a lot of beer. We also spent the night together. I wasn't in the habit of doing that sort of thing but there was just something about him, I was hooked. I loved his smile, his sparkling blue eyes, and his outlook on life.

We began to see each other regularly. Nick was taking a two year business management/accounting course and was about to begin the second year. He was staying with his mother and step-dad and I was working and living about ten miles from where they lived. We had a lot in common and as Nick said we complimented each other. We shared the same passion for dogs. He had a little Jack Russell terrier that was quite wild, and I had three dogs of my own. We also loved walking, looking for rocks, for gold, and old mines.

He was on disability from the accident and trying to make ends meet on a limited income. He also had a son from his previous marriage that would stay with him every second weekend. I have always been one of those people that likes the underdog, takes in stray animals and wounded birds, and especially admires those that make success stories out of sheer will power and hard work and Nick fell into that category with flying colors.

Nick was incredibly smart, liked 'numbers' something I am terrible at, and we would talk for hours about everything from world problems to mundane everyday events. How I loved him! We spent the rest of the summer walking, dancing at the same bar we met, and were together every minute we could manage.

I happened to be standing in line at the bank one day when I saw Nick, his son, his mother and stepdad come in together for a meeting with the loan officer. He explained to me later what he was there for, his step-dad had agreed to co-sign a loan at the bank for him to begin his second year of schooling and he had also bought Nick a fantastic laptop. He had to be the real thing for his family to believe in him so much. My love for him soared.

In September, Nick took his travel trailer to the city where he would go to college and parked it in a camp ground. This is where he would live for the school year. His little dog was a problem. He didn't like being left in the trailer all day and his barking annoyed other campers, so Nick decided to leave him with me during the week. That was a huge sign of trust because he adored that little dog. Nick would spend the weekends at my house or sometimes I would go to visit him in the city, but it was harder for me because I had to find a 'sitter' for my dogs, cats and horses.

We got along so well, I couldn't imagine not being with him. About three months in to his school year, he phoned me one night and asked if I could lend him the money to catch up on his trailer payments. It was quite a bit of money, but I knew money was tight for him, and gave him the loan. He said he would pay me back when he was working. It wasn't a problem, trust was becoming a big part of our relationship.

He had his son for Christmas that year and Christmas Eve was spent with his mum and stepdad and son. I was sad because I had spent so many Christmases alone and I had been excited at the prospect of waking up Christmas morning beside the man I loved. I was disappointed but I understood. I saw him after Christmas Day dinner, when he came to pick me up at a friend's house and we spent part of the next day together too.

Nick's schooling would be over by late spring, and he wanted to move and start over somewhere new. I assumed he must have had too many bad memories where we were now. We both decided on the north. I hate flying but I bought plane tickets to fly up to the Yukon to look at a house up there. Unfortunately at the airport I chickened out and he went by himself. Yes, I should have gone, but I didn't. Nick loved the Yukon, loved the property, and the people, the lifestyles in the North, and put a down payment on the house. As it turned out, there were some problems with the windows and insulation and we decided to cancel the offer, but were unable to have the down payment of five thousand dollars returned. It would have to be decided in small claims court at a later date. He graduated a couple of weeks later with honors, he had aced the courses and earned a degree in business management and accounting.

I had a piece of property in the mountains not as far north as the Yukon but still in the north and Nick wanted to move there. It was quite an isolated property, it had an old house that I had converted from a barn, and not much else. No water, no power and not much of a road in. I didn't want to live there but we decided to try to make a go of it. His heart was set on living in the bush, a completely different way of life than he was used to. In May 2006, we moved up there. We built a beautiful big shop for him to do 'shop' stuff in, filled it with new tools and equipment and spent the rest of the summer building barns and fencing and enjoying being together.

Nick's son came to stay for a while, and his mother and stepdad visited. He had not had a lot of contact with his dad in the past few years, and it was wonderful that he visited too. It was nice to see the two of them together, although their personalities clashed at times. They were a lot alike. He brought Nick's young step-brother with him, who was a really nice kid.

My father's suicide, only two years before still bothered me and occasionally I drank too much beer and slept at night with the help of a sleeping pill. But my 'rock' was making my life better and better. One afternoon I was looking for him and found him down at the beach, fishing. I was in an irritable mood, but when he turned and smiled, I still remember the way it made me feel. I asked him how he could always be so calm and happy. Again that smile, and he said 'he had peace in his heart'. That night there was a forest fire up the valley. The sky was bright red and glowing and it scared the daylights out of me. I wanted to feel like Nick. Peace. The next day I quit the beer and the sleeping pills.

One of the first instances of his 'forgetting' was to do with the court case for the return of the five thousand dollar deposit for the property in the Yukon. The court had decided to allow Nick to present his case by phone as the cost of the trip there and back was so expensive. The afternoon of the court case, he 'forgot' to phone and the five thousand dollars plus expenses was awarded to the owners of the property as a default. I was choked and also upset that it didn't seem to bother him, but I let it go. It didn't seem worth causing problems over. It couldn't be changed anyway. The money was gone.

Fall came and went. We got in the winter's firewood, and we were pretty proud of ourselves when the shed was full. But now we were running out of money. Neither one of us were working, his disability had long since gone. During the summer, I had paid off his truck so he didn't have truck payments anymore, using the money from the sale of my house when we moved. Still, even without payments we needed an income. He had decided he didn't want to pursue his education with anymore accounting or business courses, and didn't want to use what he already had for a career either as had been his original plan. I was a little confused about his decision but respected it. We lived 35km from a very small town, not a lot of work in that area anyway.

We pumped water from the river into jugs, used coal oil lamps for light, and kept the fire going to keep warm. Snow piled up. I had a little more money left over in an account at my credit union and before Christmas drove the 800 km distance to take it out. Nick kept the home fires burning, the animals fed but it was tough for him to be alone at the farm. Short days and long cold nights. I was back in four days and we caught up on bills, bought a better wood stove, and fixed the floor in the house to make it warmer. And then it was almost Christmas.

Nick had decided to go back to his mother's for the holidays. First he would pick up his son, and then head for a family Christmas and would be gone for a little over a week. I was devastated spending the holidays alone in the middle of nowhere but didn't say anything. We lived too far out for someone to feed animals and keep the fire going twenty four hours a day.

When he came home I was so glad to see him and hoped that was the last time we would spend Christmas apart. We spent time out in the snow, tobogganing and sledding. We didn't have a television, but instead played lots of board games together with his son. New Year's Eve came and the two of them went skating in town and blew up fireworks at home. It would have been nice to have been home for the evening after he had been gone all Christmas but he didn't get much time with his son and that was what he had wanted to do. I told myself kids grow up fast and we would have lots of New Years together.

After the New Year, things began to settle down again. His son had gone home, life was about keeping warm, shoveling snow, feeding and watering animals and waiting for spring. Once again by April we began to run out of money. I suggested he look for a job in town.

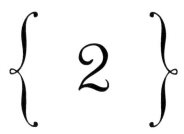

{ 2 }

WHEN I HAD MET NICK, HIS DIVORCE AND ACCIDENT HAD TAKEN everything he had. I had wanted to help him the best I could, and I loved and trusted him so I signed over the property to him for a dollar, so that he had something in his name, his bills were paid off, it was a new start for him. But now he needed to work.

Finally, right out of money and no jobs for either of us, I sold my truck to catch up on child maintenance, his schooling loan, and other bills. I had a little income coming in but not enough to live on. Again that ran out quickly, and the next option, he put a mortgage on the free title property. It was a high interest rate as his credit was still poor even though he didn't have any outstanding bills. But now we had a mortgage payment and because of the mortgage, a payment each month for house insurance as well. Nick was getting moodier and I assumed it was from the financial stress and not knowing what he wanted to do with his life.

One morning, I found him outside sitting on a bench staring at the ground. I sat with him for a while, trying to get him to talk to me, to tell me what was wrong. I finally gave up and left him sitting there. He never did explain what he was thinking and there was nothing I could do to fix it. A couple of hours later he came back to the house. He needed to have something to do as in a job. We both knew that. He just couldn't seem to do anything about it.

The next day we talked about getting sheep for the farm. Maybe this would work. The few cows we had, consumed so much feed and brought in zero income. I don't eat meat and the thought of keeping animals for slaughter made me sick but if he could make it work, and I didn't have to be involved in that part I would live with it. Sheep came. Money left. Sheep left. And there was nothing but for him to get a job.

He began to work for a Mennonite farmer building a hay shed for him. Nick was an amazing self-taught carpenter, actually he was amazing at anything he did. His talents were endless. He could look at an empty site, visualize the building and build it. He could read plans but didn't need them. He was excellent at the job and needed it to be perfect. From there he began to work for the farmer's nephew who had a construction company. He also began to go the Mennonite church. That was hard for me. Mennonite women sit on one side of the church and don't participate in the church itself. They also wear long dresses and bonnets and don't question the division between man and woman. This was something he would be doing on his own.

With Nick working, I took over the majority of the farm work. It was hard and tiring and I have never wanted to be a farmer. It also tied us down. Or should I say it tied me down.

He got up early, went to work, worked hard and did an excellent job. But as the summer went on, he began to find fault with how his boss, who was quite a bit younger than him, ran the company and the jobs. He found fault with his co-workers and the bottom line was no one could do the jobs as well as he could. I found it hard to listen to every night, because he would get so wound up talking about the things everyone else did wrong.

He still went to church. In fact, he spent Thanksgiving with the Mennonite family. I was alone most of the time and have to admit resented the time he spent with his church friends. But they seemed to fill a need in his life. I should have said more but the 'enabler' in me wanted him to be happy, and not get upset or depressed and so the 'we' part of us began to fall by the wayside as the church time increased. His moods of depression still came and went and I hoped to avoid them by keeping the peace and letting him be happy. Wrong I know, but I was brought up with two very strong beliefs. Patience and tolerance. Growing up in my father's household, fighting wasn't allowed. We had to learn to work out our differences by talking it through. The problem for us - Nick wasn't brought up that way so it was easier for me to say nothing than to end up in a fight which would have solved nothing.

Nick also began to say things that were hurtful. His mother was like that and his father too. In fact after almost two decades of being divorced they still hated each other. Some of the things his mother said about people were quite insensitive and in some cases downright mean and that is how I attributed Nick's lack of empathy to myself and to others.

One afternoon we were sitting on the beach drinking a beer. Things had been up and down and when I became stressed I had a bad habit of scratching my face. He looked over at me and said 'You make yourself uglier every day'. His voice was nasty and the look on his face was one of disgust. I had never seen him like this before. I felt belittled and hurt, but I said nothing. I didn't know what to say. Who was this man sitting beside me? That hurt stayed with me for a long time.

Though Nick was working, the payments for the student loan had slipped far past being caught up, and I assume his mother took care of paying off the loan for his stepdad. Child support had also fell into arrears as had the visiting privileges with his son gone by the wayside. It wasn't long before Maintenance put a lien on the farm. I was devastated. I don't honestly know where the money went, the bills still weren't as high as most people have. I had some money coming in, he was working but we were always, it seemed, broke. We weren't making any improvements for water or power or the road either.

That Christmas, Nick spent with the Mennonites. I was alone again, sad and wishing I was anywhere but here. He never really had an explanation for why he spent so much time there, he didn't seem that keen on the church itself and never read the Bible but not wanting to start fights and sound like a nag, I kept the peace and went along with it. By now I had seen he had a temper when pushed. He also had begun to have the dark mood as I called it that would come and go in between bouts of depression.

Sometimes I thought it was like living with two people. When he was in a good mood it was wonderful, but when he became depressed or angry he was the other side of the coin and the only thing was to wait it out until it just seemed to go away on its own. Sleep was one thing that could get rid of it and sometimes by morning it would be gone. After a while, I knew he couldn't just stop the moods, he didn't even know where they came from. At first I used to tell him – 'just let it go' or 'if you really want to get out of it you can'. Finally I began to realize this was something he couldn't control and it wasn't just a bad mood. Something was going wrong inside him.

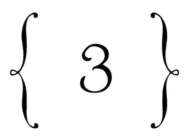

WE HAD ONE NEIGHBOR. THAT NEIGHBOR, TO BE POLITE, WAS NOT A very nice man and unfortunately he and Nick just rubbed each other the wrong way and their feud escalated. The neighbor controlled the easement down in to our property and decided to shut it off. We were no longer allowed to drive in to our farm. But Nick found a way to get an access using crown land, built a quad trail through the bush and kept us going by driving the quad up and down day after day, sometimes six times a day, morning and night, going to work, bringing in supplies, taking out garbage, all the things taken for granted with a vehicle. It would be six months before the application was approved to build a road in. He was amazing, and he did it.

One of the worst problems that happened by not having our road occurred when we hayed our field. We needed to borrow a machine to bale the hay we had cut and the neighbor had put locks and barbed wire on the old access. Nick borrowed a baler and drove it to the top of the road, where he asked permission from him to come in and bale and promised that he would take the machine back out as soon as he was done, around four or five hours. The neighbor refused. It was ridiculous of him and also downright mean. The road was dry, it would take half a day and our hay would be in the shed. The neighbor called the police and two officers came, it was a hot day, tempers escalated and the police ended up in a fight with Nick. He wound up in jail after having been beaten by the cops. A bad day all round, except for the neighbor who walked away gloating.

I had been waiting for Nick to come down the road. He had called to say that the police were coming and he would get them to let him in. I could hear by his voice he was aggravated and getting angrier by the second. I asked him to leave, let it alone. He stayed. The next call I got was from the police station. An emotionless voice repeated three times 'sell the farm' and hung up. Twice that happened and then nothing. Finally he came home. He looked terrible. They had pulled his hair out, bruised his neck, his voice was raspy and he had cuts and abrasions on his arms and face. He had also been charged with resisting arrest and fighting with the police. His court case was in the spring. This wasn't enough for the vindictiveness of the neighbor and over the winter he continued to send information to the courts trying to get Nick sent to jail.

Jumping ahead to the court case, I had written a letter for Nick, apologizing for his actions to the court and the police. It was the only way to try to get this mess cleared up. I didn't want him to go to jail. He didn't deserve to go to jail. I gave the letter to Nick, and told him to sign it and mail it. He refused, said a few inappropriate comments and left for work. Apparently he did do both, signed and mailed it. On the morning of his court case Nick was loud and puffed up with the attitude of 'don't care what they do' when he left for town. He phoned me a few hours later. The case had been dropped, the DA telling him that they hadn't thought he had it in him to apologize. The police were reprimanded for their actions and Nick walked away.

When he called me, he was crying on the phone, all the bravado when he left that morning had been an act. I was ecstatic that it was over. He was happy and relieved and so was I. He never did say thank you and I told him looking out for each other is part of life but he never said anything. Two good things that came out of it all was that the neighbor lost his plan to force us to move and Nick settled down for a while.

Church had begun to lose its interest for Nick. It just wasn't that important anymore. He had never done the Bible studies or even opened the Bible and he was at the point where he had to become a 'member' not a drop-in person, which including renouncing his sins and accepting Jesus. That was too much of a commitment for him and he decided to quit. And that was it, he never went back.

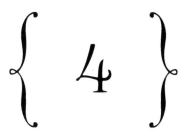

{ 4 }

I WAS ALONE WAY TOO MUCH AND I NEEDED SOMETHING TO DO OTHER than just farm work. I woke up one morning with an idea to start a magazine. We had bought three hair goats the spring before and I thought making a goat magazine would be fun for us and something we could do together. I would do the writing, he would do the graphics and the advertising. It was winter, long dark nights stuck inside and he was a computer whiz.

At first he was totally into it, actually enjoyed creating it, and he did just about all of it. And he was good at it. His computer skills were awesome, mine were terrible. His knowledge was double mine about goats and his ideas were as always, amazing. We got the first one out, and we were both very proud of it. Nick found someone to buy a printer with him, learned to work it and printed, cut and stapled hundreds of magazines for the first few months.

There was one other goat magazine in the country that had been around for many years. It was very different from what we were putting out but it had the loyal following of the goat world. We had to compete. Our magazine improved and became thicker and thicker and took more work to put together. Nick was still working, but he handled it all and seemed to thrive on it.

The first hint of problems began one night when he was working with a lot of photographs on the computer. Sometimes it just wouldn't load the information or the pictures and he became really angry. I started to say 'why don't you try' and he turned and screamed at me. This was the first of the 'new voice' and the red eyed rage on his face. I put it down to being tired, or frustrated with the computer. I made excuses for him but I was hurt, he was mad and we began to go to bed angry. Something we said we would never do. I asked him later that week if he still wanted to do the magazine. His answer was 'why, you think I can't do it?' I knew he could and he had always told me he wanted to do things with his life, that's why he had moved out to the farm. To be different and make something of himself that other people didn't do. So, I left it at that.

Nick had also stopped working for the Mennonite in construction. He had started to be later and later for work and argumentative and critical of how the work was done. He was now working for someone else building their house in town. He was allowed to go in whatever time he got there as he said he had to do chores at home. I still did the chores, he just began to have trouble getting up in the mornings and used the farm as an excuse to be late.

The magazine was a big hit because it was easy reading, a ton of information and photos and lots of stories from readers. Selling advertising was tough but it got easier as the magazine improved. It also became too big for one person to print, and so we made the decision to go to a printing company. It was expensive but the advertising should have been able to take care of it. There wouldn't be a big paycheque at the end but it would be able to hold its' own.

That summer, Nick decided to become a judge for goats. He aced the course, got his ticket, showed two of our bucks in shows, taught them to drive, so many awesome things in his newfound passion of goats. And he was excellent at it. Unfortunately he began to fight with the editor of the existing magazine and that created problems with a lot of the 'goat people'. He didn't get any judging assignments, not that there were a lot to go around and it was a politically biased group.

Nick began to back off from the magazine, he had lost interest. I ended up doing the research, the writing, the graphics, putting it together, the advertising, basically all of it and the mailing list as well. It was a full time job, and along with the farming I was exhausted. He was still the 'editor' and I wrote his editorials for him.

The magazine was nominated for Best New Magazine and he was interviewed by phone for CBC from the coast in which he did a great job. And to boot, while he was at work on a job in town. The awards dinner was in Vancouver. I was stuck here and he went with his mother. I remember him phoning from the hotel room to ask what his speech was if he won. And again from the awards dinner, asking what the answer to a question was in the current issue, which of course he wouldn't have known as he neither wrote nor read it. He had by this time removed himself from anything to do with it other than handing it out.

The magazine didn't win but Nick received a lot of praise and attention at the dinner which was wonderful for him. After all he had done the initial creation. I wanted him to be happy and even if he didn't do much with the magazine anymore, he had done so much in the beginning. When he was happy, I was happy. His mother, I assume just believed what she wanted to believe, that he was the one doing everything.

Nick worked in town five days a week and picked up the mail. By now there was an outstanding overdraft at the bank but it wasn't getting paid off. Any cheques that came in for the magazine and some were quite good, didn't make it into the business account. One day I asked him about it, and he said that he had spent his money on the magazine and that he was taking any that came in now. The magazine was in debt, we were in debt, and there was no money.

In Canada small magazines and newspapers are allowed a grant to keep running them in the black. I applied for the grant and the papers came. Nick said he would do it but as the deadline approached it still wasn't completed. I nagged him to do it. That was a mistake because the more I worried, the more I nagged, and the angrier he became. I found a person on the coast that did grants for a percentage of the money paid out but Nick wanted to do it himself. And so again, I waited and worried.

Finances were becoming our main focus, a mortgage that only the interest was paid on, a lien on the property, maintenance threatening to take Nick's bank account and his driver's license and anything else that would make him pay the arrears. Both our stress levels were maxed. Nick decided to ask his mother to help him. He phoned her and much to their credit they lent him the money to catch up on the bills. I could hear him thanking her but then he told his mother that he had filed for the grant and as soon as it came he would pay her back. The papers were still sitting there untouched. He was happy for a few days free from the stack of unpaid bills and the stress they had made but the grant still had to be done.

I wrote letters and maintenance gave him back his driver's license and bank account. But the lien on the property remained and increased monthly.

The night before the grant was due I convinced him to fill in the papers. He was angry and sullen but he did them. It was a long night, and we worked till two in the morning. Unfortunately, it takes more than a few hours of putting together some numbers out of a hat, and the grant was rejected. We folded the magazine a few months later.

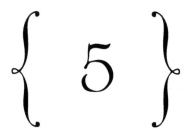

{ 5 }

When the sheep were sold, it was something that was left up to me and it broke my heart just as it did when the cows left. I knew where they were all going. We got next to nothing for any of them, and I couldn't even convince myself they got good homes. Of course they didn't. They were livestock. And now we had moved on to goats.

Quite often Nick had talked about the different things that people he had met were doing. He was impressed by the fact they could achieve so much and that was what he wanted to do. He once told me he didn't want to be ordinary. He knew he could be successful and make a lot of money doing a lot of different things. I believed he could. When I met him this would never have been a problem. If his illness hadn't been there, he would quite likely have been a millionaire by now, his ideas were unique, his skills amazing, he worked hard and he wanted perfection in the finished product. He could see things that I never saw. He had the vision that makes someone the best of the best. We worked well together, as Nick had said when we met we complimented each other and we could have had a financially successful and a happy life. But as the moods came and went, parts of him did too.

We were fencing the following spring and that was the first year Nick's angry moods became physical. The quad wouldn't start and I suggested it might be out of fuel. Before I knew it, I was laying on the ground in the mud. Out of the blue, he had pushed me as hard as he could, and down I went. I was stunned. I was hurt but not physically, and more so because he showed absolutely no remorse. He got the quad going and we finished the job and didn't talk about it. He did tell his dad on the phone next time they talked and his dad said he shouldn't do that. You think!

Nick's anger stayed pretty much just verbal for the next while until we were shearing the goats. Then he had an angry episode that came out of nowhere and lasted for a couple of days. That was also when I saw the redness around his eyes again, the dark circles underneath them and the sparkling blue color changing to that cold steel grey.

We began to shear the first of the little guys, and he was as always so good at it, so kind to the animal and ended up with a near perfect fleece. A self-taught technique, a new skill he that he had learned on his own. But that day he suddenly became angry for no apparent reason. Nothing out of the usual had happened, he was just angry. When I asked what was wrong, he threw the shears at me. I ducked and they hit the ground breaking one of the teeth from the steel comb. I was stunned, where had this come from? He took a time out and I waited. When he came back, he was quiet and still looked angry but he finished the job.

His mother and stepdad came the next day for a visit. He was still moody and just couldn't seem to shake it. He hadn't slept very well that night and his eyes still had the red look. We walked out to where we were going to shear the goats and his parents were waiting there. He looked at me and out of the blue yelled, 'I'm trying – why don't you'. I had no idea what he was talking about and was so embarrassed I didn't say anything. It was a long morning and his mood didn't improve too much. But by afternoon he was feeling better and no mention of it was made again.

In his travels to the judging clinic and the goat shows, Nick had seen how the hair of these goats could be made into socks. And expensive socks. He put himself into this with the same gusto as other projects, the socks were a huge hit and he sold every pair that was made. When he would go to the Christmas craft fairs, he loved it, people remembered him, they loved the socks and they loved him.

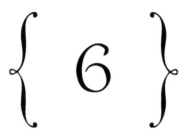

{ 6 }

ONE SPRING, NICK BUILT A POND FOR ME. IT WAS IN THE SHAPE OF A heart and we filled it with goldfish. The next year when the ice melted, I walked there every day looking for the fish, and one afternoon he was driving by and phoned me. Excitedly he told me there was gold in the pond, he had seen a lot of goldfish swimming along the surface. I couldn't wait to see them and ran all the way down there. We spent a lot of time together feeding the fish the first few summers, some of the special times I remember.

Another day we were driving along the road and Nick stopped and said, 'that tree will make the stairs for the loft in the house'. It didn't look much different than any other tree, it had a curve in it but other than that nothing seemed particularly outstanding. The next weekend he went back, cut the tree down and lugged it home along with another piece of a tree. He built the most incredible curved staircase to the loft that everyone that has come here comments on. How he saw that tree in the proverbial forest and it stood out from all the rest I have never figured out. I love that staircase and it is a constant reminder of the person that he used to be.

That summer we had a man move out here to start a homestead on the farm. He was a little eccentric and spent three months building a two story cabin that he never finished. Nick built a one story cabin in three days for the wwoofers we had coming to work on the farm. This cabin was beautiful, and the work fantastic and as always, perfect. The steps were all that were left to attach and Nick had to go back to work. The man that was staying here offered to put the steps on. All the man could find laying around was a cheap piece of wood to attach the steps to the deck, and he said it would have to be changed to something stronger when Nick had time. He also said that he knew that it would never happen. He was right, the steps finally began to fall off five years later and a friend of mine fixed them. How did this man know? I didn't.

It was a tough summer. Nick had begun to be angry about so many things, his moods became longer and the depression deeper. He would say some terribly cruel things. One morning he was in the truck about to leave for work. He was late and I had been outside doing chores for a while. As I walked up to the truck window, for no reason at all, he leaned out and yelled 'you're a fucking loser' and drove off spewing gravel behind him. I was stunned and hurt. That was the first day of the phone calls. He would phone and start screaming and swearing at me. It didn't make any sense and it would upset me terribly. If I didn't answer he would leave it on a message. One evening we had finished dinner and I was still reeling from the day's phone calls, and I said to the homesteader, do you want to hear a message from Nick?

Nick looked embarrassed and after I began to play it, the man told me to shut it off, as did Nick. I don't know why I played it but I was hurt and angry and had no idea why he was leaving these messages. But I was wrong to do that too. I should have erased it right away as I did the other ones. Two wrongs don't make a right. The phone calls stopped about three weeks later.

He also began to be late doing his taxes. Nick had made a company when we moved out here so he could write things off for the business and also his expenses from working. That was another thing that was starting to annoy me because he was so good at numbers, had taken schooling to be an accountant but never did his taxes. When we moved in together he had boxes of immaculate records. Now, pieces of paper, receipts and bills were shoved in places from drawers, to jean pockets to where ever they fell. This was not the man I met where everything was done precisely, neatly and responsibly. As the third and final notices would arrive for taxes I would freak. I would nag. He would do them with a good degree of hostility and resentment the night before they were due. And in most cases the phone calls would follow asking for explanations for the tax return because the figures didn't jive.

What was happening to this man I loved so much. But every now and again a glimpse of the smiling guy with peace in his heart that I had fallen in love with would surface and I would say to myself, 'it will be ok'.

{ 7 }

THINGS BECAME STRAINED BETWEEN US. HE WOULD BE HAPPY ONE minute and down the next. He said he was depressed about things but didn't know what or why. We decided he should see a doctor and find out what could be done to help the way he was feeling. Physically he was a fit, healthy strong man.

The visit with the doctor was somewhat predictable. He was prescribed antidepressants. That was it. No real work up, no physical work up. Take one pill a day and you will begin to feel better.

That summer Nick lost a tooth in front on his bottom jaw. It left quite a big hole and we thought it would be good to get one made for it. It took a lot of money and time but one afternoon he came home with the tooth and showed it to myself and the homesteader. It fitted into his mouth with a wire and came in a little case to keep it in when not being used. He was very proud of it and it looked good. For a while he wore it a lot but then only when going out somewhere and then not so much at all. It rode around a lot on the dash of his truck, first in the case then just sitting on the dash. When it finally broke that was the end of it and it went to the garbage bin. Everything always started out great but ended the same way.

That summer, his dad came out with his step brother for the last time. And that was my fault. Nick's truck always had something wrong with it, every light on the dash board lit up and he just didn't seem to care. When I met him, the truck was immaculate and now it was a disaster. We were supposed to go somewhere one evening and the truck didn't make it out of town before breaking down. Lights on everywhere. I was choked. I was angry and becoming angrier every day with the crazy stuff that was happening.

Nick's dad was a handful and he seemed angrier that summer too. Nick was at work and I spent the days with his dad and stepbrother. His dad had started to yell at me lots and call me names. His step brother had some emotional problems, he was a teenager and as his dad used to say, a little slow. I liked his brother and he helped me with the chores and walking the dogs. I had some people coming to pick up goats from a long distance away. We made lunch for them, his dad and stepbrother finally decided to eat with us as did the homesteader. It was fine until after the company had left, and then between the griping at me from his dad and from Nick, I am sorry to say I lost it. I asked his dad to leave. I was wrong, it was wrong, but I was so tired of all the bickering and the yelling at me from everybody. Nothing I did was right and everything was wrong. I handled it badly and that was the last time they were here.

The anti-depressants were obviously not working – in fact if possible things were getting worse. Our first wwoofers were three young Spanish guys. They hitched a ride into town and were actually picked up by someone who knew Nick. They asked how he was to work for and the fellow answered 'as long as he gets his own way he's ok'. He liked perfection and there is nothing wrong with that. That was who he was. But now he didn't care as much about having things right, having things perfect. The changes in him were becoming more and more noticeable.

Nick's little dog started spending time with the Spanish guys and slept in their cabin at night. As Nick's moods became worse he sometimes took them out not only on me but on his dog as well so it was much more fun for him with the new guys.

The first time I was really embarrassed in front of people happened a couple of weeks later. We took the dogs and the Spanish guys up the mountain to hunt for gold. Nick was out of the truck and heading up the trail while the rest of us were still getting organized. The bugs were bad and he yelled back at me 'Shut the fucking door'. I was stunned. I was hurt. I was embarrassed as the three guys were too. Hurriedly we got our stuff and locked up the truck. Nick never turned around, looked back or apologized at any time for his outburst. When we met he would never have condoned anyone treating a woman badly. In fact he made it quite clear it was wrong when he saw or heard it. Yes, things were changing.

During that fall Nick started to become forgetful and he had trouble concentrating. He went to the city with one of the Spanish guys and later the kid told me that Nick had become confused. He couldn't explain it any better than that. The man he had gone to pick up a piano from said the same thing, although not in such a kind way. He phoned me and said to tell the guy that just phoned to forget coming, and that he was a few bricks short of a load. I was embarrassed but also scared at the fact that he was not able to do simple errands like he used to. Things were becoming terribly wrong. Maybe the antidepressants were making things worse instead of better.

A few weeks later, he was again in the city and should have been home by eight or nine. He wasn't answering his phone and I began to worry about bad roads, accidents all sorts of terrible possibilities. Around eleven pm he phoned from a drug store and calmly asked what kind of toothpaste I wanted. We didn't need toothpaste, why was he trying to buy toothpaste? I tried to keep the panic from my voice. I sat up and waited for him and he arrived home about two a.m. – he was tired but seemed ok, and he was safe, that's what counted.

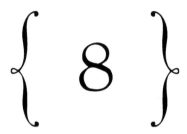

{ 8 }

That Christmas he was home. We had two new wwoofers, a young couple from Germany. They were good kids and we all got along well. Over all, it was a nice Christmas. We made a big dinner, Nick could cook a turkey in the barbecue better than anyone could cook a turkey anywhere. The strangest thing throughout their stay was the way he constantly answered me with 'Yes Honey' in a southern type accent. They asked me about it and I didn't have an answer so I made one up about him seeing a movie and picking up the accent. I had absolutely no idea where he got it from. It lasted about three weeks and then vanished as quickly as it came. I asked him once why he was doing it and he asked 'doing what'? I left it alone, better that than have him get angry.

We had decided to build a tower for wind power. I had put the foundation posts in that fall, and we built a small house on top during the holidays. Nick never made a plan, it was all in his head. The kids had hauled over a pile of 2' x 16's, and the tower was on its way up. He cut the angles he needed with a skill saw, then up he went, taking the pieces of lumber with him one at a time. I don't understand how he could visualize the structure as he went but he did. The end result was this perfectly correct tower, forty feet in the air, all beautifully constructed with wood on top of this little 'doll's house'. Wow! It looked awesome. He built the platform for the top of it, on the ground, then tied it to his belt and climbed up the ladder he had built on the side of the tower. The platform settled into place without a problem and it was finished. Nick could have been an architect and made millions, he was so incredibly gifted with a talent that came naturally.

The next wwoofer to come to our home was a woman from Germany. She was wonderful and we have remained friends to this day and she comes to visit each year. She and Nick didn't get along very well. She didn't like the way he treated me. He had begun to belittle me and would talk to her in a normal voice and then turn to me and at times be quite nasty. It was January and very cold and Nick still worked in town doing inside construction and renovations. On occasion she would go to town with him for a day out, and on one of these times she mentioned to me after that the four or five errands on the paper I had written out confused him as to where to go first. There is only one short street in town and he had trouble deciding what to do and in what order. It made him frustrated and in a bad mood she added.

I began to worry more and more about the different problems he was having. It was hard to understand that all these odd things in his life were due to depression. By March, he had become much worse. He didn't want to go to work, didn't want to do much of anything. Shearing the goats had become a chore for him, and this time we had help for the month from a woman from Hong Kong. She was wonderful, a nurse from a big hospital and had decided to take a break and travel through Canada. She commented on how Nick and I communicated. By now we had fallen into a pattern of 'sniping'. It seemed I was hiding my hurt feelings all the time and he was always finding fault with who I was and what I did. A vicious circle that never quit. To him I was always an idiot. Everyone else were becoming idiots too.

Chinese people don't say the letter 'v' and instead use the 'w'. One evening she was telling us a story about life in Hong Kong and he suddenly lost it, screaming at her about the way she spoke English and mocking her use of words beginning with 'v'. It was awful and she was hurt, I was embarrassed and he was angry but in his mind absolutely right. In the past he might have thought this if he was really irritated but never would he have openly hurt someone's feelings for the way they talked by yelling it out loud.

I thought that he should see the doctor again to help with the depression and the anger. It wasn't getting any better, in fact it was worse and other problems were cropping up. Maybe a new type of pill. The doctor he saw this time was a 'fill-in'. His diagnosis was also depression. I am not sure how they come up with their diagnoses after a few minutes of talking to the patient but they do. This doctor believed it was the result of Nick's accident years before and called it post traumatic syndrome. Nick was quite relieved and happy. That evening he phoned his mother and told her he knew what was wrong with him. The therapy the doctor prescribed was watching a video, answering questions that it asked, reading, and doing the homework with the cards that were included in the kit.

Getting him to watch the video was difficult. To be fair we tried watching it together and he was bored. I was bored. It was poorly done, situated in Scotland, the accents making it hard to understand what they were even saying and to have to relate to the people in the video was a tough one. He fell asleep. He had begun to do this if there was something he didn't want to do. One morning I gave him his tax forms and five minutes later I looked over and he was asleep holding the papers.

A few days later Nick had a really bad day. Moody and angry. I was bringing in firewood and the woman from Hong Kong offered to help and asked where Nick had gone. I said he was watching his video to help him work through a bout of depression. When I came in he was sitting at the desk, head down, asleep with the laptop playing the video. That was the last time he picked up any of the material to do with the post traumatic syndrome theory. Even if he had had the PTS, it would have taken a lot more than just sending the patient home with a video and instructions on how to 'cure' yourself.

The next week he went back on depression pills, with a higher dosage.

{ 9 }

OUR NEXT VISITOR WAS A KID FROM BELGIUM AND A LADY FROM Italy. As it turns out, this nice lady was taking a break from her life where she lived just outside Rome. She had been married twenty years and one morning her husband looked at her over the newspaper at the breakfast table, and said he wanted a divorce. She had just been released from her job as an airline hostess with a good settlement and he was a bus driver on a low income. But she was bi polar and living with her just wasn't what he was capable of handling anymore.

It was tough for her and as she said he was the nicest, kindest man but she was just too hard to live with. She was still in love with him and she didn't blame him for leaving. She stayed on her meds for the most part of her two month stay here, but now and then her moods would get the better of her and she would say some quite nasty things that hurt a lot of feelings. She also told me that she knew Nick was bi polar too. I didn't believe her. I didn't want to believe her. But I began to do research on it, I think mainly to prove she was wrong.

It was a tough summer, his moods were up and down, he began to hate work some days, didn't want to go in, didn't want to get the hay in, but there were some good days too. We carried on and the good days were wonderful and outweighed the bad ones.

Little jobs that he could do so easily before began to annoy him. When they didn't work out he became frustrated. His concentration was not as good as it used to be and one day he was trying to take the tire off a wheel. He repeated the same process over and over and nothing was working out. I stopped for a minute on my way by and suggested he try a different way. A second later he had thrown the tools, luckily in an opposite direction from me. There was a window standing against the post by the shop and he looked at me with such hate and yelled, 'I should shove your head through that piece of glass'. I wanted to cry but I didn't. I walked away. What else was there to do when he was in that mood? Getting into a fight or standing there bawling my eyes out wouldn't accomplish anything.

We began selling eggs to offset farm bills. I was looking after a couple hundred chickens and he would take the eggs to town on work days. This was something he loved to do and he had a lot of happy satisfied customers, but for me it was work and a lot of it. Feeding, cleaning sheds, washing eggs, getting cartons ready. He got more and more customers and as he promised them, the eggs were the best in the valley. We fed the chickens well, and adding a lot of scraps from the grocery store in town made the eggs even better. The hay crop was good too. He had learned to farm with the same amazing talent he had for everything else in his life, everything but our relationship and the business end of things.

That summer his parents asked him to go fishing at the

ocean with them. He had gone the second year we were here and he had really enjoyed going. A lady had contacted me about a few hair goats she had that she needed a home for and I asked if he could pick them up on the way back. We were using more hair to make more socks. He was excited about the fishing and it would give him the break he said he needed and not a problem picking up the goats.

The last night after fishing he phoned and said he would be on his way as soon as they had eaten dinner, he would see me late the next day. That was the last I heard from him until he arrived home – in the middle of the morning two days later. He said he had just been driving. Our dog was really ill and needed to go the vet and Nick had the only vehicle we owned. Quickly we unloaded goats, loaded up the dog and he left again. It was such a panic and he didn't get back until that evening. I asked him why it had taken him so long to get back from the coast. He was understandably tired so I left it at his answer of driving and having to have a sleep. Somewhere though he had lost about a day.

September came and shearing time. He used to get quite excited about shearing because he was good at it and the results were an awesome amount of hair that we had made into socks and he loved wearing and selling the socks. We were taking a break from shearing and sat down in the lawn chairs by the shop, drinking a well-earned beer and enjoying the last of the summer sun. I can't even remember what we were talking about, when he suddenly went quiet. A few minutes later, he became angry. He jumped up, and I followed him, asking him where he was going. The next thing I remember I was laying on the ground. He had hit me, choked me, and threw me against the shop wall. As he walked away he kicked me in the ribs. I laid there for a few minutes getting my breath back. I heard the truck start and he backed out and was gone.

He had smashed my cell phone and it laid in pieces on the driveway. I walked to the house, but stopped halfway as I saw the internet cable on the outside wall cut in half. I had no transportation, and now no communication with the outside world, and 35 km from town, the nearest neighbor two km away but the one that had tried to send Nick to jail. Now what?

I was okay and more worried about being left with nothing than by what had happened. The minds way of coping with something awful I guess. I didn't sleep much at all, I kept thinking that I heard the truck coming home. By morning and still no Nick, I knew I had to start figuring things out. How was I going to get to town, find some money – he had the bank card – was he ever coming back? He had taken a few clothes, not many and some personal stuff. I found an old cell phone and I called the phone company and amazingly enough lucked out. Apparently you don't need the phone to be activated with them for them to answer. I gave them my number and asked if I could switch this phone to it. They said sure, my knees went weak with relief and I wanted to cry. Within minutes I had a working phone. The laptop was useless as the outside cables were cut in half and I had no idea how to reconnect them.

I suppose I should have called the police and reported what had happened. Abuse of any kind should not be tolerated for any reason at all. Do I regret not calling? No. Would he have got the help he needed and finally a doctor that would have diagnosed his illness before it progressed as far as it did? Probably not. The system has more failures than positive outcomes. Nick was already unpopular with the cops in town so what kind of a chance would they have given him. I am not making any excuses for his behavior but I also know that he had things going on in him that made him do things he had no control over. This wasn't the person I used to know. But he should never have physically hurt me, that was unforgiveable.

I called his mother, though I didn't tell her what had happened, and she said nothing so I figured he hadn't called her. I called a friend who lived three hours away and she said if I needed anything they would bring it. I told her I would give it a couple of days but at least now I knew me and the animals would be okay. And then I waited. Two days later he phoned. I still don't know how he thought he could call me when he had trashed the phone. I guess he forgot parts of what happened and of what he did. He wanted to come home. I was happy, go figure. I should I have just said 'get lost' after what he did but I loved him and just wanted the whole thing to go away. All the time he had been gone I also worried that he might have sold the farm and taken the money and run. I didn't know. The situation was becoming impossible and I didn't know how to fix it. I knew the way he had been acting wasn't him but that didn't make it right either. I started to worry about him even getting back, maybe he would have a blackout something like the fishing trip and end up who knows where. I know I should have been worrying more about me than him. But I wanted him to come home. I hoped we could get him the help he needed to get better and get back on track. It wasn't fair to me and it certainly wasn't fair to him to be losing himself like this.

He had made it all the way to the coast before he ran out of money. He had sold some socks and had enough money to get home. While I waited I thought how great it would have been to have been doing this trip together not the way he had done it. I also worried about what I would say to him when he arrived home or what he would say to me.

Nick arrived home the next day. He never actually said he was sorry. He did bring me a rock and say if he did it again to hit him in the head with it. Later I threw it in the river. That was just too weird for me. I said it would be okay, he looked embarrassed and I kept my emotions hidden so that he would feel okay too and be glad to be home. We didn't talk about it or why it happened or anything that we should have. He never said what he had been thinking about while driving or even why he wanted to come home. He wasn't overly loving or affectionate, he was just home. He fixed the internet cables without a word. The whole thing was laid to rest but it should have been the beginning of counselling for both of us and another trip to the doctor. It should have been the start of trying to really figure out what was going on. The next time he did go to the doctor a couple of weeks later he told him what had happened. The doctor's answer was 'you can't be doing that', 'take more pills', so much for the doctor getting us into counselling or trying to figure out why a man would lose his temper and his control like that. When Nick told me what the doctor said I was choked. No help here.

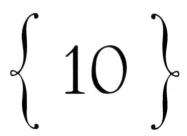

{ 10 }

Nick took a few days off after he got back but eventually
returned to work. He had to explain where he had been, so he
just said he had to go away for a few days. That fall wasn't good.
It was also the beginning of worse times ahead.

A couple of weeks later he again was having a tough time
getting up to go to work. He said he wasn't feeling good at all.
He had pains in his chest. After numerous visits to the hospital
and ambulance rides to the city, and tests of all types, they ruled
out any heart problems or other serious illnesses. Diagnosis - he
had anxiety. His mother had a heart problem, he didn't. I am not
sure where his mother came up with the idea he did too, but this
was the beginning of a lot of interference from her that caused
even more problems between Nick and I.

Nick began to carry a jar of aspirins in his pocket to take for
his 'heart problems'. The doctor had suggested it and it seemed to
make him feel better. He was laid in bed one Saturday morning,
the heart pain bothering him too much to get out of bed and help
do chores, though he had been sleeping quite soundly when I

came in. Around eleven a.m. his mother phoned. She had phoned the night before but he wasn't home at the time. He had stopped in to visit someone. She asked him how he was and where he had been the night before when she phoned. He explained and she asked if everything had gone okay during the week. His answer was 'he didn't get heart attacks when he was talking to people'. He stayed on the phone quite a while, sitting up in bed, talking and laughing and he was right. He didn't seem to have any problems at all. I went back outside disgusted with the whole thing.

The past couple of years, Nick had been having a lot of accidents with the truck and his insurance was climbing. It was already high from the single vehicle accident he had had before I met him. All of these latest were single vehicle accidents as well, usually hitting moose or deer, he said. This time he rolled the truck on a corner of the gravel road he had driven hundreds of times. The truck was a write-off. It was mid-morning and he phoned me from his cell phone and told me. He wasn't hurt, the little dog wasn't hurt but the truck was finished. He got a ride home and came in as if nothing had happened. I said he should at least phone his boss and tell him he wouldn't be in for work. As he was explaining on the phone, he was laughing. I couldn't understand how he thought rolling the truck was funny. I was choked. I was angry. He could have been killed, and we no longer had a vehicle and lived 35 km from town.

But as luck would have it, he was able to borrow a truck from a couple in town. They had a farm truck that he could use until the insurance was settled and he could replace the one we lost.

He got a ride back to town to pick up the loaner truck and I took the dogs for a walk to calm my nerves. His mother phoned, he had phoned her but she had been out. I told her what had happened and she was understandably upset. The last truck he had written off had almost cost him his life. His step dad was also on the phone and his mother said to him, 'you talk to her I can't talk to that woman'. I was hurt but tried to explain how it had happened, that Nick was ok. His mother began yelling from the background that I should have packed my belongings in a wheelbarrow and left with the homesteader weeks before and some other things that made no sense. It was awful. It had been a horrible morning and the day wasn't getting any better. I finished my walk and went to bed until Nick got home. My stomach hurt, my head ached and I was tired of everything.

Nick was quite happy go lucky for a few days, the insurance was settled quickly, he could pick up a cheque in the city and go truck shopping. Another farmer, was heading up that way and offered him a ride to the auto dealerships. Within a couple of hours he phoned and said he had found one, but it would cost a little more than the cheque he had for the insurance claim. It was however, a diesel, something he had wanted for a long time. The extra fees were for the warranty, taxes and insurance and he bought it. The extended warranty ended up being invalid after the first couple of months because he never bothered to keep up the maintenance on the truck or send the receipts in either by email, fax or mail. A letter came a few months later voiding the warranty. It was sad to think this truck was on its way to being a junk pile like the last one.

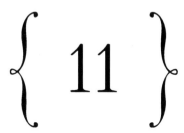

{ 11 }

NICK WAS WORKING ON AND OFF, HAD SO MANY MOOD SWINGS AND another increase in the anti-depression drugs. I was stressed to the max. I felt terrible and looked awful. I didn't know how to fix things, the doctor didn't help, didn't seem to even care. One day Nick said to me he had seen a woman in town he knew and she looked fifteen years older. Before I could stop myself I answered with 'maybe her husband yells and screams at her every day'. I could tell I hurt him and I was sorry for what I had said – I never used to say nasty things but I was starting to act the same way he did and I hated myself for it. Later we learned her daughter had a terminal cancer, I felt so sad for them and more determined to fix things for Nick and I. We weren't dying, we could do this.

By now I had been doing a lot of research on bi-polar. It all fit, and I asked him to talk to the doctor to see if he could get a referral with someone who would maybe have an answer how to help him. Our small town doctor said that the only place he could go would be to the coast and he couldn't give him a referral for there. That was a pile of BS because two hours away is a city full of medical resources for mental illness. We took the doctor's word for it though. Just keep taking these new antidepressants. It was over and done with just like that, there was nothing wrong with him but that he was depressed. What a joke. No help or answers were coming from here. I was angry this time, no one seemed to care about what was happening to this man I loved. It wasn't fair to him and it wasn't fair to me or to us.

That summer at haying time, we had had one load of bales left to get in but had to leave it for the next morning. It was getting dark, the dew had settled in and the bales were getting wet. We decided to get up early and finish it as the clouds were rolling in too. The next morning, I went out at six a.m., did the chores and checked the hay bales. It looked like rain wasn't too far off, but the wind had come up in the night and dried the dew from the bales, and that gave us a chance to finish the last load and get it into the shed safe and dry. By now it was seven and Nick was still in bed. I tried to get him up but I could tell by his face, he was in 'the mood'. He had the red rims and black smudges, the grey eyes and his face set in anger. He sat up and looked at me and I knew we were in trouble. He was nasty and told me to 'fuck off' and laid back down. I said I would get things ready. I went outside, drove the truck and trailer to the field, went back in and he was still lying in bed. I tried every-thing to get him up, bargaining by saying he could go straight back to bed when we were done, that it wouldn't take long, I tried making deals, anything to get him up. Finally he flipped, jumped out of bed, and pushed me aside. He was dressed in minutes and by the time I got outside he was roaring down the field with the truck and trailer. I ran behind and caught up as he was throwing the first bale on the trailer. We were half way done when it started to rain. We kept going and later parked the trailer and tarped the wet bales.

The more it rained, the more the new road with its base of clay would be turning to mud. We needed to return the mower as soon as possible to the farm on the other side of town that we had borrowed it from. Nick was wild by now, hooked up the mower and took off. I ran behind the truck again, the one km up the hill. He had made it through the worst part of the road but was stuck at the narrow culvert. He was livid. When he was angry, reasoning went out the window. I tried to help him, but whatever I did or said made it worse. We were both covered in mud and it was pouring. Finally we got everything unstuck and were able to move again. I guess he drove the shit out of the truck because he was angry. He took off dragging the mower behind him with a piece of the truck falling off, left behind in the mud. I walked home disgusted. None of this should have happened. If he had just got up, everything would be done right and he would be back home already. We could have been sitting in the nice warm house, with a big dry stack of hay in the shed. Nick got home later that afternoon but stayed in a lousy mood for the next couple of days.

Two days later he went to work, the sun was shining and I had to take all the wet bales from under the tarp, put them in a building, cut them and spread them out to dry. What a ton of back breaking work for him being in a crap mood. When we first started to hay, he loved the way the field looked after baling, was proud of the stack of hay we had and was already planning and talking about how to improve it for the next year. How things had changed.

Moods were happening on and off every couple of days.

Nick was getting worse, and the moods lasted longer and longer. Sometimes he would sit in his chair for a day without moving, or looking up, nothing. Then he started sleeping in it, spending his nights there. I phoned a counsellor but they said he had to phone himself. Fat chance I had of convincing him to do that. I asked him and got the answer I thought I would. There was nothing wrong with him, it was me.

I decided to call his mother and ask her if he had problems with moods and anger before. As always she said there was nothing wrong with him and insinuated I was the problem. I gave up. It would always be my fault.

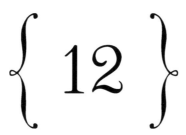

$$\left\{ 12 \right\}$$

THAT FALL JUST BEFORE HIS BIRTHDAY, NICK TOOK OFF AGAIN. HE spent two days without speaking, just sitting, and then moved into the spare room. He wasn't working much, not doing anything on the farm, just sitting. He said he was leaving. He spent another day packing, sorting clothes, muddling around with his stuff. I asked him where he was going, and tried to talk to him. He wouldn't answer. That night I tried again to talk to him. He was laid on his bed, just staring. Finally, he looked at me and said, 'Getting the fuck out of here, why would I want to be with something like you.' The look on his face was hate and disgust. I went to bed alone and cried.

The next day he got up and spent a few hours getting his stuff together. He didn't want breakfast. He wasn't hungry. I tried again to get him to stay, make a plan or see the doctor again. He lugged his stuff out of the house and was leaving but the truck wouldn't start. A couple of hours later he got it going. I tried to talk to him again. He just sat hunched over the steering wheel, the engine running, staring at the floor. I knew I was going to cry so I turned to walk away and he roared off, the truck blowing blue smoke all the way down the road. I didn't think I would ever see him again.

A friend had been staying in the guest cabin and he offered to get supplies from town, we still had only the one truck which he had taken, and sick to my stomach, the farm was still in his name. The only way to have added my name to the property was to catch up on the maintenance lien for his son which we hadn't had the money to do. This time I freaked. I really didn't think he would come back. A hundred animals to feed, nothing legally in my name, and who knew what he would do now.

I called my friend the next day. The same one I had called the year before. She was as always there for me. She had also been telling me for a long time to leave him, she knew someone with bi polar and Nick was just like him. They don't change she said. How could I walk away from everything with nothing and leave behind all those animals and hope that Nick would take care of everything if he did come back when he couldn't even look after himself. Besides, I honestly didn't think that he would be back.

She came down the next day, with two friends. They brought bags of groceries for me and the animals, they bought a bunch of stuff I was selling so I had cash, and bought the majority of the laying chickens. There would be no way I could make egg deliveries without a vehicle and she said she had been looking for chickens and was going into the egg business anyway so may as well buy mine. What an awesome friend. After she left it hit me how alone I was again and I wondered if this time it was permanent.

The next morning Nick phoned and wanted to come home. He had only driven two hundred km before he ran out of money.

He was home by afternoon, his mood was good, and he said he knew this was where he wanted to be and with me and that it was forever and would never leave again. He never offered a reason for why he had to leave, never said he was sorry for anything that had happened and I didn't push it. It would have led to a fight and not likely any type of answer anyway. He never had answers and never wanted to talk about things. That morning before he came home, I had phoned about finding a counsellor in town, but we apparently needed a referral from a doctor and the doctor still didn't think there was anything wrong with Nick. It was the same old circle, no one wanted to take the initiative and point us in the direction of the help we needed.

The friend in the guest cabin had his parents visit from Europe. It was Nick's birthday a few days after he got home, and we had a party for him. It seemed to go okay and he seemed happy. A couple of days later he told me that after everyone left, and I was asleep, he had walked over to a cabin in the bush a little ways from home, took a gun with him and thought about shooting himself. Thankfully he didn't but it left me shocked at how miserable he really was. Would the doctor like to explain this one?

He went to work for a few days and had asked around about finding another job other than the renovation work he was doing. A guy he knew phoned while he was at work and said he had a job for him. The job was a couple of day's construction at a mine, but while there he could look around and maybe get hired on permanently with the company that drilled for them. I was excited that this might be the thing he needed and assured the man I would have Nick phone back.

That night he was in a terrible mood. He went straight to

his 'room' and laid on the bed. Twice I went in and suggested
he phone the guy. He became angrier and angrier and I became
angry back. After a few rounds of yelling he finally phoned, a
time was set up, and he was to leave the next day for the job. He
put the phone down, turned over and went to sleep. I went to
bed alone and miserable. We should have been celebrating this
opportunity not angry with each other.

By morning his mood was gone and he was excited. He was
happy and he packed what he thought he needed to take with
him. I dropped him off in town for his ride and he phoned me
four times along the way telling me where they were and asking
how I was doing.

Three days later he was hired full time by the drilling company itself and was ecstatic. The next day he left for work. The
friend that stayed in the guest cabin offered to drive him to the
city to catch the ride into camp. When he packed his gear, Nick's
little dog was excited and thought he would be going too. It had
been raining and he jumped onto Nick's equipment bag. His feet
were a little wet and Nick went nuts. He threw him off and that
poor little guy was heartbroken. Nick went in to the shop and
grabbed a rag, rubbing dry the paw prints that were left behind
on his bag. He turned to us, and yelled, 'What's wrong with you
fucking people'. That was the last thing he said to me as he left. I
felt like shit and at that time I was glad to see him go. In a couple
of days I was missing him.

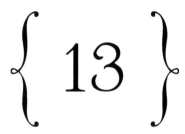

NICK LOVED THE JOB AND WAS AS ALWAYS GOOD AT IT. HE LOVED THE camp. Things went pretty good and a couple months later he had two weeks off for Christmas. Usually he was gone 24 days and home ten. I was looking forward to spending the holidays with him. He had seemed to be in a pretty good mood, he was still taking the anti-depressants, and maybe these new ones were finally working.

A week before Christmas we bought a propane on demand hot water heater. Nick promised to have it hooked up and I would have my first 'bath' in years, maybe we would even have one together. I was excited. We also picked up three big puppies that my friend's dog had in October and she couldn't find homes for. Nick fell in love with the puppies especially the biggest of the three, the black one. We called him Tika, meaning Little Bear.

Things seemed to be going okay, but the hot water heater was on hold, he needed more fittings and so it would have to wait until after Christmas. We cooked Christmas dinner to-gether, took pictures of the puppies and went out and cut down a little tree. Together we decorated it, and it was beautiful. Nick always cooked the meat and the turkey was doing its thing in the barbecue. He was a master at it. By five o'clock it was ready, along with the potatoes, vegetables and stuffing. He made the gravy and it was perfect. Two bites into the meal he announced it tasted like shit, and it was always the same thing, smelled better cooking than it tasted. I looked over and he had the red circles around his eyes. No, this can't be happening I thought. I didn't say anything, he didn't eat anything and about an hour later he went to bed. Christmas was over.

The next day the mood was still there but much worse. He spent the day finding fault with everything. I had also brought home my girlfriend's young black cat, which she had just neutered. He had been a barn cat and needed some time to become associated with our other ones. In particular he picked on the little black and white female Rexy, who Nick really liked. All of our animals are spayed or neutered and this new cat was still wanting to mark his territory. I had told Nick it takes a couple of weeks to lose the male instincts. The two cats had met in the shop and the little female was screaming. She made a lot of noise whenever anybody looked at her and this was no exception. Nick ran in and went crazy. He hit the black cat with a board and knocked him out. He thought he was dead and threw him into the back of the quad trailer parked outside the shop. I was sick to my stomach and screamed at him. I went back to the house but just before I got there I heard a cat screaming again. Running back to the shop, I could see him leaning over the trailer. The cat had regained consciousness and Nick had a knife and was trying to slit its throat. I went nuts, screaming and crying. It was like a horror movie. He yelled at me 'get the fuck out of here if you don't like it'. He killed the cat and stuffed it in a garbage bag. The mood stayed for days and I couldn't bring myself to even look at him. He never apologized or explained. He never spoke about it. He never apologized for anything he did and this would be no exception. If he thought blame should be there it was always someone else's fault and theirs alone. It would begin with 'You did, didn't, used', etc. and no blame was ever put on himself. It was a horrible Christmas and I was glad when January came.

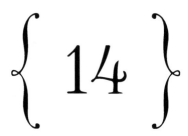

I KNEW HOW BADLY NICK NEEDED HELP. IF HE HAD BEEN COVERED in sores and boils, or he had lost his hearing, or his legs wouldn't work, I would have taken him to see a doctor even if he didn't want to go and the doctor would see all the obvious physical problems and would have had to figure out what was wrong with him. Visual aids. If you can see it you can fix it.

I had phoned the doctor in town twice before that fall but got the same answer and no one took me seriously. It takes time for the anti-depressants to work he said, although two years was looking like a hell of a long time for results. I phoned the crisis line but I apparently wasn't the one with the crisis. That I thought was a debatable issue.

I know a mental illness is hard to diagnose and exactly what is wrong even harder, what is causing it – another problem, and other than actually witnessing an angry episode or seeing the depression, the person looks perfectly normal. First the doctors have to believe the possibility of something more than just de-pression. The symptoms were there, but the doctors wouldn't listen to him or me or consider for one second that it wasn't just depression. But even 'just' depression can cause physical side effects or suicide. Depression that had gone on this long was obviously not 'just' depression and the anger and violence was an added factor. One doctor told me it would be my word alone that he was acting mentally ill and asked me how my partner would feel towards me if I was trying to get him committed. I wasn't trying to get him committed, I was trying to get him help. I hadn't even considered the fact that he would have to go to a hospital and stay there. I thought it was a twisted answer, a way to stop me from annoying him anymore.

Nick should have gone back to work the first week in January, but no one called him. Finally he phoned his boss and asked when he would be going back. A week later he called again, but more excuses were given. I suggested he phone the next day and find out what was going on, everyone else was going back. Eventually, his boss said there was a problem in that Nick had been telling the guys at work that one of the employees was the worst driller ever and couldn't do his job properly. This man happened to be the son of the guy that got him the job. For some reason Nick had taken a real dislike to him and told the rest of the employees all the things he thought the man did wrong.

He looked absolutely devastated after the call ended and finally he told me what had been said. I felt terrible for all of the people involved. I tried to explain to Nick that it was an awful thing to do to anyone. Even if you don't like the guy or he really doesn't know how to do his job, it wasn't his place to talk about it. I pointed out it was also the son of the man that got him the job. I tried to get Nick to understand. But the bottom line was regardless of anything else, I explained, it wasn't his place to gossip about anything to anyone and gossip ends up hurting everyone. It was happening just like before when he worked in construction.

We spent a really glum week. Not only was he depressed about it all, it didn't look like he would be going back to work. I asked him to phone and apologize, it was the only way to try to work things out and to be adamant that it wouldn't happen again, and mean it, I added. Nick wanted to work there so badly, but apologizing was not part of his nature. Finally one morning I handed him the phone and just said it. 'You want the job back, phone and apologize.' Seconds later he grabbed the phone and called. After the first awkward few minutes everything went well and he went back to work two days later.

Things seemed to go along okay for a while. My birthday was in March, spring was coming, and my girlfriend from Germany was coming to stay for two weeks. Nick would be away at work and that was a good thing because they didn't get along very well. He phoned me on my birthday, but the phone call ended up being a bust, he was in a grumpy mood, and as so many times in our life together he yelled 'fuck you' and hung up.

My friend knew how upset I was even though I said nothing. It was days before he phoned me back and again he never mentioned it or said he was sorry. I sometimes wondered if he thought I had absolutely no feelings. And yet on the other foot, one wrong word to him, and he would let you know for a long time how badly he had been treated.

April 1st was an amazing day. Nick came home the night before and we went out to do chores together. That in alone was wonderful, he wanted to be home and looking after things outside. His mood was good. I carried the bucket of feed to the

ponies, and suddenly I screamed. 'There's a baby pony in here'.
The year before Nick's palomino Shetland stallion had bred his
grey mare, and it had never looked like she was in foal even a
month before when we trimmed her feet. Now standing beside
her was a baby pony, the prettiest and healthiest little thing I had
ever seen. Her proud mother stood beside her. Nick came running and the smile on his face stretched from ear to ear. 'I told
you she was pregnant, you didn't believe me.' He laughed. No I
hadn't. Before meeting him, I had spent most of my life working
with horses and this pony never once looked pregnant. He had
been right all along.

Nick carried the baby and the mother followed them in to
another barn with a large fenced area. He was like a proud dad.
By the end of the day, he told me her name was Miracle, because
she was a miracle pony. He was right, not only was she a little
miracle but the happiness in Nick was a miracle too. He spent
his days off watching her play, run, eat and sleep. He was calm
and relaxed and the baby became friendly, loving and trusting,
all the qualities Nick had when I met him.

{ 15 }

Things were up and down, sometimes good moods, sometimes bad, sometimes depression. He had his anti-depressants changed again but it didn't make any difference. On one of the good days that he was home from camp, we were on our way to town and I was playing the song, Walk the Line. I asked him, 'would you walk the line for me?' You know that was the best day I had had in years. He turned to look at me and smiled, 'what do you think I do every day?' For him that was romantic and for me wonderful, and at that moment I loved him as much as ever. The feeling I had was the same when he played the two stuffed puppies on the pink pillow. When I first met him I gave him this gift and the puppies sing "I Got You Babe" (Sonny and Cher). Nick would often squeeze the button on the pillow as he passed by the toy and we would listen to the song together and feel the love we shared.

Early one morning in August, Nick had just got off shift and phoned me. He was livid and screaming so loudly I could barely make out what he was saying. He said he had had a fight with his foreman during the night for trying to take the work truck away from his drill to another job. He had flipped out and wouldn't let anyone take it. The whole thing made no sense, the foreman was angry, Nick was wild. What a mess, I was sick to my stomach. I tried to calm him down but he hung up on me. By now the moods lasted longer, and could be meaner and more irrational. He called once again before his stint ended at camp but we only talked for a few minutes and the incident wasn't mentioned.

His mother and stepdad came for a visit while he was home. He told them he would meet them in town after he went to see his boss. He told me too, that his boss wanted to buy some of the socks we made and he had to drop them off at the office. He and his parents came back to the farm later that day, and we had dinner. They had a good visit and finally about nine o'clock they were on their way. Minutes later Nick gave me a letter from his company. He was on notice for wrecking equipment, endangering employees and hostility towards his superiors (foremen). I was choked. How had he pretended all day that the reason he had to go to see his boss was to sell socks and not for the reason it really was about – this letter.

I asked him what had been happening at work. He explained it was partly to do with the truck incident, but that he had had mechanical problems with a drill he worked on and that he had exhausted a helper to the point that the man's back gave out. He was really upset and with no idea what to do, how to make things right. I looked at the letter and suggested he write one of apology. I ended up writing it, he signed it and he went back to work. I enabled him to get through another problem, but the real problem wasn't getting solved. I knew things were getting way out of control, he was getting worse not better. Sometimes he didn't even remember the things that happened or could see how out of control they were.

Fall came and still no hot water heater hook-up, the fridge had been broken months, and we were coming into winter. Nothing ever seemed to get better only worse. We had little to no firewood. That was something Nick had used to love doing and took pride in it, now it was one more thing he had lost interest in and we even had a brand new wood splitter. He didn't talk as much as he used to about work, I could see the spark was gone there too, but he told me he still liked his job, maybe it had just been a long year.

One night before leaving for camp, Nick was pumping water while I did the chores. I came up to the house and there was water pouring everywhere. He was inside with a flashlight in his mouth trying to hook up a battery to a pump to fill up the tank for the hot water heater but the hot water heater was still not ready to use so it wasn't even logical. His bag was half packed, stuff laying everywhere. He was trying to do so many things at once and not getting anything done and making one heck of a mess in the process. He seemed really happy, almost too happy. I helped him finish with the water, we put the other stuff away and he spent most of the night waiting to go to work the next day, not much sleep at all.

I found it so exhausting. All these mood swings, the worrying about what he would do next, would he be able to keep his job, trying not to upset him. I was stressed out and I had never been so tired in my life. I just wanted a normal life, not living on the edge, not living from mood to mood, just being happy and living a peaceful life with him. That was something that seemed to have disappeared long ago. I knew it was getting worse and

I didn't know what to do about it. I had looked up so much information on line, made my own diagnoses, asked him to see a doctor but now when I tried to talk to him about it he would say there was nothing wrong with him, it was me. I decided other than an intervention what could be done and I am pretty sure an intervention wouldn't have worked either, it was a desperate thought on my part. Many of the days that he had at home now were spent sitting in his chair, just staring. He became angry at nothing, his appetite was down and he had trouble sleeping. I would ask him if he was coming to bed, and he would sit there, staring at the floor, no answer. I would go to bed and he would still be in his chair in the morning.

Christmas shut down came early in December. His last shift finished late afternoon and the guys took the camp truck into the city and as per usual were given a motel room for the night. He hadn't called by mid-morning, and I tried him at the hotel to see when he would be getting a ride home. He wasn't in his room and I started to freak. Around one o'clock I finally tracked him down in another room, hung over and in a miserable angry mood. He hung up on me three times while I tried to ask if he was coming home, if he was okay. He phoned back around four, and said he didn't have a ride. I told him I would buy a bus ticket and pick him up in town later that night. He agreed so I bought the ticket by credit card. I called back but no answer. Finally he answered the phone an hour later and said he didn't need the ticket, he had a ride.

It was a long drive home for the four people in the truck, as he puked most of the way. The friend staying in the guest cabin offered to pick him up, it was snowing and cold, and I was relieved not to have to drive to town that night. When Nick came

in he was still in a terrible mood, threw his gear down and went
to bed. I was told he had puked all the way from being picked up
in town as well as on the way from the city. I was glad it wasn't
me driving.

By around noon the next day, Nick was feeling better and
managed to crawl out of bed. He looked terrible. He also had
the red rims around his eyes, the dark circles, signs of the angry
mood. Years before when the moods had begun, they usually
only lasted a day. By morning they were gone and we would
wake up and I would ask him 'is it over'. He would answer yes, he
would never say sorry, but I would cuddle up to him so happy to
have the guy I loved back. But that was then. I should have never
let things go this long, hoping things would fix themselves, or
doctors would have answers, anti-depressant pills would finally
work. I blame myself for not getting him the right help and getting him better before it had gone this far. I should have tried
harder to find the answer. I know he wouldn't talk about things,
about the moods or how he felt, because he couldn't understand
it himself but I could see what was happening, why couldn't anyone else. I should have found a way to get him to the right doctor.

The Christmas party was two weeks away. I didn't want to
go, I was afraid to be out with him in public in case he turned
on me, embarrassed me with some of his comments or fell into
a 'dark' mood and flipped out. I took the coward's way out and
I stayed home and he went with our friend who had just started
working at the mine as well. Nick looked awesome in his good
clothes and I felt the pain of missing being with him, going places
with him, having fun with him, of being his 'woman' like we
had been in the beginning. I asked him not to drink a whole lot,
he still was having trouble remembering the 'party' two weeks

earlier when he had been so sick. It had taken him along time to come out of that mood and he had been depressed for days. That was still worrying me.

The next morning after the party, the same thing happened as the time before. He wasn't answering the phone in his room. No one knew where he was. Apparently he had a few drinks, and a few more and so on, had a couple of arguments with other employees, and then went to the downstairs casino with everyone. He was found lying in the hallway on the wrong floor hours later. Someone put him in another room where he slept it off. When I finally talked to him he sounded fine, but didn't remember a whole lot of what had happened the night before. The two of them arrived home that afternoon. He seemed quite happy but I was still upset. He never used to do things like this. What the hell was happening? The next few days before Christmas were a nightmare. He was angry, then depressed, then angry and depressed at the same time. Friends came and he barely left his chair. He wouldn't look at anyone, talk to anyone and constantly had the hood of his sweat shirt pulled down over his eyes, even in the house. I didn't see his face for days, he slept in the chair and barely went outside. I was scared, I was angry and I didn't know what to do. The more I looked up things on line the more I was convinced he was bi polar. Who did I call that would believe me? Not his family, not his doctor, no one believed or wanted to believe he needed more help than he was getting with those stupid anti-depressants. He just got worse and worse and there was nothing I could do but watch. I felt like I was losing my mind.

A few weeks before he had begun telling people that the moon was getting bigger and bigger and was going to crash into the earth wiping part of it out. At first it was just me he told, but then when on night shift at work he began trying to convince co-workers it was getting closer and the end was coming. I remember the looks on the faces of the people visiting when he tried to convince them too. They thought he was joking, but when they didn't take him seriously he became agitated and then angry and then sunk back into the depression. It was an awful visit and the tension in the house was terrible. He believed about the moon, for him it was real. I phoned his doctor and said I had been looking things up and I told him about Nick and his moon theory and could it be a psychotic episode. I could hear the annoyance in the doctor's voice and his answer was, 'maybe you don't give him enough of the right attention'. I hung up. What an ass.

{ 16 }

ON THE TWENTY THIRD OF DECEMBER, NICK WOKE IN A TERRIBLE mood. Somehow he had driven the truck into the ditch the night before and needed to get it out before the snow plow came and had to get by it. He left on the skidoo but came back twenty minutes later. He had pulled it out but had left the power on the day before and the battery was dead. He was livid. I was choked. The snow plow driver had called and said the truck was in his way. Nick was angry and sat in his chair and I went back up the road to take up battery cables to boost the truck and get it moved out of the way.

When I came back I couldn't find Nick. I started to make breakfast and still he didn't come in. Finally I decided I had better look for him. As I grabbed my coat from the door I saw one of the guns missing from the rack. I felt cold and sick inside. I dropped my coat and ran outside in the direction of the place he had told me he had been going to do it before. As I passed the barn, there he was sitting on the ground bracing the rifle butt and he had the barrel beside his chin. That was the way his brother had killed himself years before. I remember screaming and ran to the guest cabin to get help.

I couldn't do anything but walk circles with my hands over my ears to block out the sound of a gun going off. I was crying and shaking and I left it all up to our friend to talk him out of it. I am still ashamed I ran away but maybe it was a good thing because he convinced him to put the gun down – maybe he would have used it if I had been the one talking to him. I still wonder. In the house, Nick sat and wouldn't speak. Between the two of us we talked him into getting help. He actually seemed relieved at the end, and changed his clothes before we left for the hospital in the city.

The roads were terrible, the snow was terrible and it was freezing cold. We took the little dog and he sat quietly on Nick's knee all the way there. He knew things were wrong. Three hours later we arrived at the hospital. Eight hours after that he was seen in emergency. The waiting room was full and it took a long time for his turn. There was a kid at the door taking names, and when I would go out to warm up the truck for the dog, I would ask him to watch Nick and to not let him leave. On one of the trips outside I phoned his mum and told her what had happened. Her first response, 'what did you do to trigger that?' I was to blame, what else was new. I said I would phone back when I had more news.

We sat for another hour in a room waiting for the physiatrist on call. Finally he arrived. It took an hour and a half and he was very thorough and asked what seemed like a million questions. Now and then he would ask Nick why he was laughing, and Nick would answer he didn't know. At the end of it all, he sat back and said, 'you are bi polar. What was your doctor thinking, the anti-depressants could have killed you'. Yes, I thought, they just about did. Nick laughed again, the doctor asked why. Nick looked at me and said 'she told me she thought I was bi polar months ago'. All I felt was sick. It was true. Everything I had read about bi polar I didn't want him to be but now we knew. I had to leave him there and his room still wasn't ready, but where we were sitting was across from the security guards office and I asked one of them to please watch him. I had three hours to drive, it was already ten o'clock and still snowing. One of them pulled his chair into the hallway and told me to go, drive safely and not worry. Nick would be fine. I got home at three am.

Our poor friend was half asleep keeping my fire warm, had done the chores, fed the dogs and taken care of everything including stopping Nick from shooting himself. I started to cry. Everything finally hit me. And I had left the love of my life in a psychiatric ward hours from home and had no idea what would happen next. I was exhausted - mentally and physically.

I slept on and off for a couple of hours and was up and on the phone to the hospital by seven o'clock. The nurses assured me Nick had a good night, probably better than mine she said. Yes, she was right about that.

I called Nick's mum to tell her he was staying for a while at the hospital. I got her cell phone and she was already on the ten hour drive out here. I told her I would be taking up some things for him later in the day. I called his dad and explained, they didn't want his step brother to know anything.

By the time I had done as much of the chores as possible it was already mid-afternoon and getting dark. I didn't want to overwhelm our friend by leaving him everything to do again. He had generously offered to stay over for the holidays to help me with the farm and give me time to see Nick. I was so incredibly grateful, what an amazing offer. By the time I arrived at the hospital, bad roads again, his mother and stepdad had been and gone, and were staying at a hotel a couple of blocks away. Nick looked pretty good. He seemed calm and peaceful, better than he had in months. He was wearing the hospital clothes, and I had to leave the bag I brought for him at the front desk. Everything had to be checked and only given out if it was acceptable by their rules. I also took him a sock full of presents I had bought for him and a picture of the big dog he had fallen in love with, Tika, the puppy from the Christmas before. It was Christmas Eve, and when I finally left, I felt so lonely and sad. Another terrible Christmas. The drive home was awful, it was a full moon and cold but had at least stopped snowing. I counted twenty three moose on the way home. There is a story that on Christmas Eve the animals can talk, I imagined the moose saying prayers for Nick and that made me feel better.

The next day, Christmas Day, I couldn't get back up there, I had to pump water, find firewood, and everything was piling up. His mother was there for Christmas Day and I was so grateful he had company. He and I talked on the phone and he sounded good.

The next day, his mother and step dad left and stopped in on their way home. It was an awful visit. She said a lot of not very nice things, and his step dad said that they knew his brother's girlfriend had killed him but they just couldn't prove it. It was awful. My old horse that I had had for twenty eight years had to be put down just before Christmas and Nick and our friend had buried her with the tractor. His mother said that was the reason he did what he did, that was the trigger, and it was my fault. Nick was awesome with the animals but he didn't have any deep feelings for my horse, I did though. They didn't stay long and it was a relief when they left. I felt horrible for days, there would be no help coming from his parents in any way. Someone had to be blamed for what Nick had done and it couldn't be him being ill. I understand grief, I don't understand having to blame. I know that working together and helping each other through the tough times would have made things a whole lot better and easier for everyone. I was hurting too. But his mother couldn't see that, she didn't want to. I loved this man, and yes, he was her son. And it was all my fault.

I didn't have time to visit that week, it was a three hour drive one way if it was good weather and good roads, and with about five hours of daylight and a million chores to do on the farm and winter weather it was just about impossible to make it for visiting hours. His mother phoned me a few days later and said, 'what do you do all day?' I was polite but didn't say too much. She made me feel like shit.

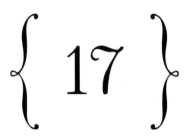

{ 17 }

Nick had an awesome doctor. She was wonderful. She would phone me every day, ask me how I thought he was, how he sounded and she would tell me how she thought he was doing. He also had psychosis along with the bi polar, she said. I knew that from the moon story that he had believed was so real. Now he thought someone was stealing the food from his tray, taking half of his sausages, and the overhead vent in his room was dirty and sending bad air in. She would help him deal with this and he would be okay.

I visited him one evening and he was great. The next time I visited, the doctor wanted to talk to me. There was also a social worker in the meeting room and she asked me a lot of questions about family violence, physical abuse and was I afraid of him. No, I wasn't afraid of him I assured her, but I was afraid of how long he had been ill, of whether permanent damage had been done to him, of whether he would get better. They both assured me he was now getting the help he needed. After all the years of the moods, the craziness, the not knowing, that was all I could feel - relief. And how much I loved him and I told them that.

He had been given a pass for two hours and we went to McDonalds. He seemed agitated, which his doctor had commented on before we left the hospital. It would take a while to stabilize the moods she said. After eating, we went to the shopping mall. He wanted to go to the Boxing Week sale, he still thought it was December. It was now January and he had missed a week of his life. I tried to explain but it left him depressed and when I took him back to the hospital he looked so sad it broke my heart to leave him there.

Nick's meds included lithium and a drug to treat the psychosis. The first one upset his liver, the second one seemed to work. That drug was Resperidone. He responded well to it and he seemed a changed man. He was getting happy, doing things in the ward, talking in group, leading group, enjoying therapy and actually helping people. The change in him was wonderful. He said a lot of nice things about the other patients in the ward. He gained quite a bit of weight but that was, we figured due to being cooped up all day with no real activity. He had day passes and came and went obeying curfews and rules. He was amazingly happy. Everyone liked him, and I was so proud of him.

A lot of back ground history was done while he was there, a lot of tests to see if he had had any brain damage that could have been caused from his truck accident years before when he hurt the nerves in his leg. They did a lot of tests to make sure he had no physical problems that could have caused his mental illness. Everything was ruled out. The bi polar was what it was – bi polar.

Nick phoned me from the hospital one day, and told me that I wasn't to worry anymore, that all the stuff about the moon had been in his head and the moon wasn't getting bigger and it wouldn't come and destroy the earth. I could have cried, it was the nicest thing he had said in months. It took a lot of courage to accept that it had all been part of his illness and to care enough about me to tell me. His voice was like it used to be. Things were getting better and better.

Finally he was released and I picked him up in the evening. He had been waiting all day and I had so much to do I couldn't leave until late in the afternoon. I regret not running to meet him and hugging him but on the long drive there I started freaking and all I could think about was what if he didn't hug me back. Really stupid on my part, but I was so afraid of being rejected and hurt the way I had been for so long. What a coward I was. I should have had counselling with him while he was still at the hospital so we could work through all the things that had happened and knew how each of us were feeling.

He told me he had made four friends, and had their phone numbers, something he had never done since I met him. Everything is going to be okay. That night in bed we held each other all night. It was so wonderful to have him home.

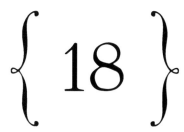

{ 18 }

THE MEDS THAT NICK CAME HOME ON WERE FOR DEPRESSION AND psychosis. There are always side effects for drugs. Even just an aspirin can cause problems which is why it says 'read the label before using'. If a person has cancer or any kind of disease which requires long term care, the meds, the treatments and the side effects are openly discussed with the people involved. Mental illnesses should be handled the same way.

Resperidone worked well for Nick, he came home read books, did chores and built a hot tub, in which we spent a lot of evenings enjoying the stars. We were happy, he still had moments of confusion but overall he was doing well and getting better each day. We went to an auction and bought two little wild donkeys. When they came home they were so scared that they would run if a person came near them. Nick began to work with them and within a week, they were halter trained, followed him around anywhere and could be brushed by anyone. He hadn't spent his life around animals like I had but just as with

most things he had a natural gift. He had also become kind and
loving again.

The same visitors that had been just before Christmas came
again and couldn't believe the change in him. They thought he
was awesome. And he was. Unfortunately the medication he was
taking had side effects of weight gain and putting a damper on
his libido. I wasn't told anything about that and I don't know if
he was either. The libido part of our life wasn't happening and
Nick decided to ask his doctor if he could prescribe him Viagra.

Nick went to counselling in town once a week or once every
two weeks, and the psychiatrist made his visit once every two
months. The local GP doctor said Nick would have to wait for
the psychiatrist to give him the pills. Unfortunately, when the
psychiatrist did show up his answer was to change his meds to
Abilify. They didn't cause these side effects.

From there life went into the tank. Nick and Abilify just
did not mesh. Within a week after being on it, he began to
get depressed again. He became irritable and didn't want to do
anything. Everything was a chore, he stopped reading, stopped
doing much of anything. He didn't even want to be in the hot
tub. He had always loved the greenhouse and the garden, and
especially the hot peppers we grew. He would put them raw
on everything, the hotter they were the better. That spring he
couldn't have cared less if we planted a garden or the greenhouse.
In fact he barely went in there throughout the year and I threw
out all the peppers before winter. It was becoming all like it was
before only there were no good days. He chose not to work part
time for his old boss in town, he just lost interest in everything,
me as well.

The stress of the past several years was catching up with me.

The new med Nick was on and his complete turn-around back to the dark personality opened up old wounds and sprang new ones. I didn't know how to talk to him anymore, he was so angry and seemed to hate everything.

My mother had died from complications from rheumatoid arthritis, an auto immune disease. I had inherited the gene, but it had remained dormant throughout my life – until now, and it finally came to surface. I was unable to walk, to move, the pain was incredible, and I had high fevers and coughing. Nick would have to almost carry me off the bed. I choked back bottles of arthritis pills, advils and anything else I thought would help the pain. Nothing did. Finally I went to the doctor, the first time in years. He knew right away what I had, and the test confirmed it. A person's RH factor in their blood should be 14, mine was 967. He prescribed prednisone which controlled the inflammation and the pain and meds to control the arthritis.

Flare-ups came and went and eventually after seeing a specialist, it was decided that I would have to go on injectable methotrexate once a week and six pills a day of various shapes and sizes to keep it under control. For a while it helped but when my stress rose, the inflammation and flare-ups went along with it, and prednisone was prescribed again. The high dosages of steroids I had to take made me crazy, and they also caused me to retain water. My face looked like a pumpkin. No wonder Nick couldn't stand the sight of me. Physically I felt terrible and looked even worse, emotionally I felt broken.

By now Nick had pretty much decided he didn't care about anything. We had a wwoofer from Belgium, a nice kid who had just finished school. As Nick's moods got worse he asked me if Nick was bi polar. He could see Nick doing things and saying things which reminded him of the way his father had been. His father had been bi polar too and had killed himself a month earlier. It was hard on him seeing Nick like this but he tried his best to do whatever it took to make things okay. It was back to that. Keeping the peace, not rocking the boat. Our same visitors came back and they were shocked at the change in him again, in only a few weeks. They couldn't believe he was back to where he was the year before.

If we had been in counselling together I could have explained what was happening right away as it started and maybe Nick would have had a chance to see it too instead of just feeling horrible. I phoned his counsellor quite often when things were really bad and she said she would work with him and see if things could improve. She mentioned that in his counselling sessions he never said a whole lot, if we had been going together I could have explained the problems he was having, we could have talked, and got everything out in the open. I know he also needed the one on one counselling too, but we also needed it together. I was frustrated because things were getting out of control not better. I would ask him how counselling went, ask what she said, how he felt, and I made things worse. I was having problems dealing with his moods again and I needed the counselling with him as much as he needed it with me. He needed to understand why I was getting so frustrated. I was angry at the way he talked to me, the way he treated me, the way he said he hated his life, blaming everything around him for his unhappiness. I lived with his illness but I was left out of anything to do with it. He should have had a change in meds, the Abilify was the wrong drug for him. The meds are supposed to suppress angry emotions, they weren't doing that, they were suppressing his ability to function but the anger was still there. Suppressing the brain and natural thought process takes away the power of everyday reasoning. The brain is a muscle and like any muscle it needs to be worked on a regular basis so it doesn't waste away. I was angry with the doctors and counsellors because just as before no one listened to me, and no one was helping and I had to watch him slip away again.

{ 19 }

NICK NEEDED A PURPOSE IN LIFE. HE HAD ALWAYS BEEN A HARD worker and now needed something to keep him moving forward not sitting day after day becoming more and more discouraged and depressed. Only weeks before while on Resperidone, Nick had put a motor back into a tractor, now he was frustrated and angry because the simple task of changing the ink in the printer eluded him. He began to have trouble sleeping. The Abilify didn't help him relax and he was so wired by night he would lay awake staring at the ceiling. I would ask if he slept, his answer 'I don't know.' He was prescribed sleeping pills. The sleeping pills turned him into a crazy person. He became angry and violent. His mood was terrible and never ending. His speech became slurred and he had trouble walking. I took him into the doctor's office and it was one of the worst days of my life. Four people in that tiny little room, and he was fuming about the 'fucking farm', 'I was a stupid fucking idiot' meaning me, among other things. The doctor had him try to walk a straight line, he couldn't do it. The sleeping pills were stopped and he was to try to sleep without them. What a joke. When we left the counsellor followed us out and told him that if he felt violent he should stay in a room in town until he felt more under control. How ridiculous to think he would be okay enough to make that decision on his own, I hadn't brought him in because he had a headache. I drove home and all the way he screamed insults at me threatening to sue me, kill me whatever came in to his head. Once out of the truck he staggered to bed and slept for a day and a half.

My feelings were so badly hurt, my nerves at the snapping point, and nothing was being done to help Nick. I phoned the counsellor and she said she would have to talk to the psychiatrist next visit. A week later he was still not himself, his speech still slurred and his concentration non-existent. We had three guys staying to help us hay and with the extra help it was done quickly and we put away an awesome hay crop. We had fertilized that spring when Nick was still on the Resperidone and feeling good and his choice of the natural fertilizer had made a huge difference.

He was parking the machinery back in the sheds when he just totally lost it. Screaming and swearing, slamming the gears on the tractor, the three guys and I kept out of the way in between catching dogs and moving them to safety. Even after everything over the years I was still embarrassed. I quietly told the guys he never used to be like this, but I don't think they believed me. Still they said nothing, and we helped push machinery around till it was parked somewhat haphazardly but under cover.

A few days later Nick decided he was going fishing. He got his income tax cheque back and bought a bus ticket. He spent eighteen hundred dollars in four days. The fishing trip was a bust, he spent two of the days in a new tent he bought and the other two in a hotel room, watching TV and eating pizza. I had said I would come and pick him up and spend a day with him but he caught the bus home instead. He came home angry and depressed. Nothing had changed.

In September, Nick finally saw the psychiatrist again. I went with him and explained the problems. I was angry by this time and fed up with everything that was going on. I was so tired of being hurt, the verbal abuse was constant. The doctor never seemed to remember who he was treating, and when he asked if I was his wife, I was so angry I said I was his friend. It was awful, and Nick was so hurt. I knew I hurt him but I didn't change my answer. Besides when was I treated like a wife? I never knew why he couldn't see how much he hurt me. I couldn't understand how it was all so one sided. I was told by a friend that Nick was narcissistic. I was beginning to believe this was true. He felt no empathy for me or anyone else. Life was about him, no one could do anything as well as him and he was the only one that was right. Most of the time I was shit to him and he didn't have a problem telling me that. The doctor's idiot answer to the problems was to double his Abilify. You have to be kidding me.

Now things got so far out of hand, it was beyond belief. Nick couldn't even explain what was happening to him he was so out of it and there was no one to listen to me. I phoned his physiatrist one day at his office in the city but he wouldn't talk to me. I tried explaining to his counsellor what was happening and she said she would talk to the doctor, but nothing happened, nothing changed. He stopped showering, shaving, cleaning his teeth and she would have to tell him he had to shower at least every two or three days but he didn't. I thought it was because he didn't want to be near me. Later I learned that it was a sign his brain wasn't working properly and it wasn't him doing it intentionally.

Since he had come back from fishing he was sleeping in the spare room again and our life together was basically none existent. Nick was miserable. I was miserable. We got a TV so he could watch sports. Then for his birthday I changed the plan to a hundred channels. At first the TV was in the other guest cabin. He would go down and watch it for hours. Then as it got colder we hooked it up in his room. The friend in the first cabin was tired of the bad feelings that filled our home and decided to move on. I don't blame him at all. I would have loved to run away too but I couldn't leave.

Earlier in the summer I finally made a deal with maintenance to buy out the lien on the farm, and the way I did it, I screwed up. Should I have done it where I added my name to his, I don't know, but Nick took his name off the property and I think that was something he never got past. It was back in my name but with a big mortgage on it. I had lived for eight years with just his name on it and it had been okay for me. He felt differently. But if he did disappear again, what would I do if he couldn't be found. He wasn't doing well at all. It was back to that, I handled it wrong, counselling would have explained both sides to us and it would have been done properly. Yes, we should have been in counselling together. This way it caused hard feelings for us both and I hurt him terribly but unlike me he always held a grudge.

Nick hadn't worked now for almost a year, he didn't really want to do anything but watch TV. We needed firewood, but I was too tired and felt too ill to nag him about cutting some so we bought it from a Mennonite. This man worked in logging twelve hours a day, cut firewood on the side and raised five kids. Nick slept most of the day away or watched TV. It was embarrassing. He had just given up and nothing I could say or do made a difference. Most of the trips home from counselling, he would scream and yell at me or not speak at all. I am not sure what went on behind those closed doors but it wasn't working. She also said it was her opinion that he had given up. I told her that he needed more help than he was getting, that saying he had given up was not the answer. Could he see someone at the hospital in the city, a referral to a doctor there that could take the time to really talk to him, change his meds, anything? I asked her again if we could do that and her answer was 'some people just never get better'. Right, and how could they if they were zonked out of their minds on drugs, I thought, the wrong drugs? But she added, she would mention it to the psychiatrist. I never heard back. Nick became even more depressed spending a lot of time sitting in his chair or laying on his bed.

Winter set in and I hate winter at the best of times. It was long, cold and dark and this year in our small house it seemed to be oppressive. Nick wasn't even interested in helping with chores. Now and again he would but wasn't happy about it and made his feelings known. The double Abilify made his brain slow. It was bad. I looked up so much information on the internet and I knew he had to get off this drug. The psychiatrist wouldn't be back until January, he was away holidaying or something, and I was scared that it would be too late. I phoned a lot of other places, therapists, homoeopathics, anyone I could think of but they all said he would have to wait till after the holidays. I asked them if there was anything I could do in the meantime and I am sure they thought I was a pain in the ass and told me there were no answers. I was so worried about what the drugs were doing to his brain. No one seemed to care. Nick was just a case number to them. I was pissed.

During all my calls I found a group couples therapy course in the city. We went to the orientation but it turned out he needed a different course first. The group would have been good for us later. When I asked Nick why he wanted to go he answered, 'to help you learn to relax'. I guess the stress was showing more than I knew but this was the first time and the only time he ever mentioned it. I wish he had said more, opened the door for talking but it didn't happen. He also never said what the couple's course would do for him. I guess the answer for him was all about fixing me.

Nick had decided to spend Christmas with his mother and stepdad. I was miserable at the thought of being left alone again but didn't say anything. Maybe getting away would help him. I bought him a pile of Christmas presents and filled his Christmas sock for him to take. It was almost like the year before. I drove him to town, the bus left at 11: 00 pm. We stopped at the gas station for a coffee and lottery tickets. We were standing at the counter and I asked Nick what else he wanted. I don't know what he was thinking about, and without even looking up, he snarled 'fuck you' at me. The man behind the counter was choked, I was upset. It didn't even seem to register on Nick what he had said.

About three months before this, we had been going to take a trip to the city together, and we had stopped at the same place as now, for fuel. Nick was wild because I had asked him not to drive with two feet, something the Abilify drug he was taking had caused him to do. It was scary when he had one foot on the brake and one on the gas pedal. Nick blew up at me, and almost rammed the vehicle in front of us at the pumps, got out, threw the keys at me across the hood of the truck and screamed some insults. It was awful and unfortunately all caught on video. We went straight home that day canceling our trip. Nick was in a terrible mood the rest of the night and the next day. Two days later I was in town and a stranger came up to me and told me that I didn't have to take abuse from any man. I was so embarrassed, the man meant well, he had seen the incident at the gas station and wanted to help. I said everything was fine and left it at that. I pushed it away, hid it along with all the other things that my brain wanted to forget, things that eventually would make me do and say stupid things. Counselling together would have worked this out too or at least got it out in the open.

And now here I was at the gas station again, two days before Christmas, and he was swearing at me in front of people. Nothing changed. The weather was awful, the roads bad and the bus still hadn't come by three a.m. so we went home. The next night I took him in again and this time he finally got on his way to his parents.

Christmas was horrible and lonely. Déjà vu - Nick was as ill as he was last year when he took the gun outside. Christmas was a blur of painful memories and if I had had enough of the sleeping pills my doctor gave me the week before I think I would have taken them.

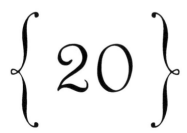

{ 20 }

FINALLY NICK WAS ON THE BUS HOME. I HAD BEEN DOING LOTS OF thinking and I was so excited and had plans to talk to him about getting counselling together and couldn't wait to show him how much I cared about him. He was to start a course in managing a mental illness once a week and I had told myself over and over things were going to get better because it was a new year, last year was gone and we wouldn't repeat the same mistakes. But he came home with pneumonia, so sick he left his presents on the bus and instead of the wonderful homecoming I had planned I took him to the hospital in town. They kept him till afternoon, and I drove back and picked him up. He spent the next five days in bed. Life just didn't turn out the way I kept hoping or planning for.

The second week in January, Nick saw the psychiatrist. I was so proud of him because he finally told the doctor he thought the Abilify was destroying his brain. Yea, for him. The outcome was another med change. Never did the doctor have enough time to actually talk to Nick about how he was feeling, what was in his future, all the important things that someone needed to have to get going again with their life. The first five minutes were spent trying to figure out who the patient was and the rest of the visit was forty five minutes to an hour consisting of 'how do you feel?' and a lot of typing on the computer. The new drug would be Seroquel. Abilify would be decreased, Seroquel increased, until the changeover was made. As the doctor cautioned, a quick changeover could cause serious problems.

There wasn't much change at first but a week later, Nick woke up in an incredible mood. We did all sorts of things together. He was laughing and talking and happy. It was wonderful, I loved him so much and he seemed to love me. The new drug must be working. Six days later he woke up more depressed than he had ever been and back to being angry and sullen and not interested in doing anything. I didn't have any idea of what was happening but it couldn't be good and so I phoned his counsellor. She in turn phoned the psychiatrist. Apparently he had a hypo-mania. When I told him what the counsellor had said, he was even angrier and more depressed. It was terrible, he had been so filled with hope too and he had been happy. I remember him stomping back to the house and I went into the shop and cried. Here we go again.

And that pretty much was that. From then on, Nick watched TV even more if that was possible. He began his course in 'managing a mental illness'. I took him into the city for the first one. He was nervous and quiet but he made it through and he seemed to get a lot out of it. I took him twice more, he did the homework, but stayed pretty quiet at home. Then he started taking the bus in the morning the day of the course, and spending the day at the center where the course was. At first he used their computers and he sent in a resume to different drilling companies. He was still looking forward. By the end of the course his depression had increased on the new drug and he was watching TV at the center.

On Valentine's Day he brought me home some chocolates. He hadn't given me a present in years and this was so wonderful. It was the next morning when he gave them to me, we had got in so late, and I made my stupid plans to have a wonderful evening, but by afternoon his mood had changed and he was getting cranky, went to bed and watched TV.

Then one day he stopped talking to me altogether, he stopped eating dinner with me and he very rarely helped me with the outside chores. He made himself a stranger to me. I dropped so much weight, couldn't sleep, barely ate, and felt terrible. Winter hung on, long and cold. I had thought to myself how I would like to check in to a hospital and get the hell away from all of it. But I knew if I was hurting inside he had to be hurting more and I watched the wall around him getting thicker and thicker. I couldn't get through to him anymore. Sometimes I just wanted to hold him or hug him but I was afraid of being yelled at or pushed away. He wouldn't let me in.

I tried talking to him one night while he was laid on his bed. I got the nasty stare and the 'what would I want to be with something like you for again'. I went to bed. He continued to watch TV, and would occasionally turn it up on the nasty parts of the shows he was watching, for my benefit I figured. His little dog spent hours laid beside him on the bed, days and nights, protecting and comforting in his own way. If Nick got up that was the only time the dog would, unless I put a leash on him and took him outside for exercise. When we got back, within minutes he would jump onto the bed again. He knew things were bad.

One day Nick decided he was leaving again. He packed a bag,

I took him to the bus in the morning and he went into the city. He would go to his meeting after he found a place to stay. Nick ended up staying at a homeless shelter. Later he told me how hard it was there, and it had scared him quite badly. I had sent him an email the day he left and said he was welcome to come home if he changed his mind. He took me up on it and after his meeting came home on the bus. When we got home, he was really happy to be there, and I asked him how long he was staying this time. His answer, 'forever'. I wanted to believe so badly. The next day he was happy. No moods, no anger, wanted to help me and was talking to me. We even went to town later in the afternoon.

That evening was good, we talked a little, then he watched TV, everything was okay. It was good. The next day, we did the chores together, and then after lunch, we listened to a cd of the Who while we painted the kitchen. It was incredible. It was wonderful. It was so normal.

At four o'clock it was over. His mood went back into the tank. By evening he wasn't talking anymore and laid on the bed in his boots, coat and hat till the next evening. He then told me he should burn the house down or himself. He had an appointment with the psychiatrist the next day in the city. I took him to the bus and he didn't even say goodbye. He was angry and sullen. I worried all day. I even sent an email to his doctor explaining that the new drug was as bad as the Abilify had been and could he help him. I explained what had happened and what he had said and asked him not to tell Nick that I had told him about burning the house down the night before. Finally Nick phoned me mid-afternoon. Nick said he had gone off his meds three days before and that he was on his way to the ER. That was all the doctor had recommended. He also knew that I had told his psychiatrist about the burning thing. What an ass that doctor was telling him what I had asked him not to. What would it accomplish other than stirring up hostility between Nick and me? Trusting or respecting doctors was becoming more and more difficult.

{ 21 }

I felt sick to my stomach. I had loved being with the person he was for the last two days, and I hadn't even known he was off his meds. Now I understood why he went off them and how he must have felt. He had been feeling real feelings like he used to. Now it was over, he would go to the hospital, they would give him more drugs, keep him there, make him feel like shit again. My heart broke for him and for me too, for us. But maybe this time they would get the drugs right, get his therapy right and he would be on his way to coming home and we would be together and this time it would be the way it should be. I phoned him and he said he was still there, he hadn't seen a doctor yet. I couldn't stand the picture I had in my head of him sitting alone in the ER waiting room. Later that night I called the ER and they said he had been admitted and was waiting for a bed. They were really nice and later on that week I sent a thank you card to them for taking care of Nick while he was waiting.

The first doctor he had this time was also wonderful. She phoned me often, and tried Nick on a new drug. She felt really positive things were getting better. Nick had told her he knew he had hurt me, he wanted to get better, and he was feeling a lot better, the new drug was a good one. We were talking, he sounded happy. He went to his meeting on a day pass and said it went well. A week later, he had to go off the new drug. It was affecting his liver just as the other ones had. But this time there were no others they could try. The doctor was also going back to the coast, her stint there was over.

Nick was still on lithium and he now had the same doctor that had diagnosed him the year before. He dropped that down to 900 mg and no drugs for the psychosis. Then Nick stopped phoning me and emailing me. I had been asked to give him some time to work through things. The last couple of times he had phoned he had been moody and hung up on me. This upset me terribly and wasn't good for him either. I sent the email that the doctor told me to send. The year before when he had been in the hospital this never happened. We were talking every day and we were looking forward to him coming home, he asked about his dogs and what was happening here. This year he didn't want to know anything about anything. The doctor said it would take a while to get all the drugs out of his system, it would take time for him to be his old self again.

I believed and so I waited. I cleaned house from top to bottom. I cleaned and cleaned and I painted. Between doing all the regular chores, extra winter chores, trips to town, and trying to make a living, household chores had been lost in the shuffle. And I am a lousy housekeeper on the best of days. I bought a new bed for us. I threw out the old junky furniture and made extra space, just made a whole new home to come back to, a new start, positive changes.

His emails became moody and dark. One said he would not be coming back to me or the farm. I just sat and cried. I talked to the doctor and was told he was working through things. Then his email said he was trying to have positive thoughts not negative thoughts and it wasn't anything to do with me. But it was obviously, or he wouldn't be having negative thoughts at all. Then he wrote that he had been offered a job where his family lived. To be offered a job I guess you have to be looking for one there.

I phoned his doctor again and again leaving messages to call me and finally the day before Nick's discharge from the ward to the group home the doctor phoned me back. He told me that Nick was happy and smiling and watching hours of TV and he would be home sooner than he had anticipated. He also told me, I presume for my benefit, that he sympathized with me, that he knew living with someone with a mental illness could be very stressful. He cut the conversation short – that was it. But the last visit he saw Nick before he left he told him that I was afraid of him. He didn't go into details about what I had really said, that when he was on the Abilify his moods had scared me and he didn't offer to see us together to explain anything. He was as untrustworthy as that other idiot. What was with these psychiatrists? They loved to tell things when asked not to or say things that should be addressed when both people are there so that it can be talked about together and understood how it was meant to be said. I decided they liked to cause shit, why else would they do it. It made me wonder if they weren't somewhat psychotic too.

By now Nick was becoming colder, his emails less frequent. Then nothing. He didn't return my calls at the group home. I left a message on his cellphone. Nothing. Finally I got a phone call from the group home asking if I knew his whereabouts. I can't even describe the feeling that came over me. The woman hurriedly reassured me that she believed he was fine but that he had left and asked if I knew where he had gone. I couldn't even talk. I just said no and hung up. I sat down and looked around at all the changes I had made in the house. Everything I had done for his homecoming. New beginnings, new starts for us both. And he had gone without a word. I was exhausted and started shaking and crying. I don't know how long I sat there but it was dark when I finally got moving again. A week later he emailed me to tell me where he was. All I could send back for an answer was 'ok'. I couldn't eat or sleep and felt completely lost. Everything we had been through, I had been through, I had stuck by, waiting and hoping for him to be well again was for nothing. I was nothing, I had failed him and had failed me/us. Nick had been saying 'nothing changes'. It only changes if changes are made but it takes more than one person to make the changes. To make the changes he wanted he would have had to explain – talk to me. Or maybe what it was, he wanted to get rid of me.

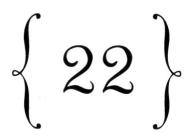

I KNOW THAT AFTER YEARS TOGETHER PEOPLE DO CHANGE, THAT IS a given, we grow, we want different things, we have new ideas. That is what keeps us alive, and it keeps us exciting to each other. Couples also go through hard times, and when they love each other it makes the love stronger. I know Nick loved me and I loved him. I still do love him. I don't know what he feels now, a couple of weeks after he left he sent me an email saying he still loved me and always will. I hang on to that. Now he doesn't talk to me or email me. He gave up everything we had worked for, he gave up me, his dogs, his home and his life to move away and start again with nothing. Every day and most of the night because I seem to never sleep, I try to understand what went wrong. I found a therapist and that has been the anchor in my life.

I struggle with the physical illnesses in my life that have progressed rapidly because of the stress. Living in physical pain all the time doesn't help and I am trying to sell 'home' because it is too hard to be here alone. This was where Nick wanted to live.

He loved it here, and then he used it as an excuse for everything that went wrong. We could have moved at any time if that is what he wanted. We could have moved anywhere. But he never talked about that ever.

I don't know how he is doing, if he sees a counsellor, takes medication, if he has ups and downs. In an email he said his reasons for leaving were that we drifted apart because of the haying, shearing goats and a bad muddy road, none of which actually made a lot of sense. We could have moved at any time or changed anything we were doing. I know his mother and step dad had been telling him that for years that he shouldn't live here, but that was his choice to move here. Not mine. And it wasn't their place to interfere. If they had been a big part of our life I could have talked to them about how Nick was doing over the past few years and maybe they would have been able to help get him better long before things went so bad for him. After nine years, he also could have left in a decent way if that was what he wanted.

Nick being gone is not a relief, and many people and doctors have told me how lucky I am, that take it as a bonus. Yes, they are probably right, but if I felt that way then I wouldn't have been trying for so long. When you love someone and you know they are hurting you try to help. Turning away was not an option for me. I was brought up to do the best you can do.

The mistakes throughout the years from start to finish, of the doctors prescribing anti-depressants, PTS videos, wrong meds, to 'travelling psychiatrists that have only an hour once every two months, to interference from parents whose agenda was not to help but to hurt was a miserable mess . A big problem throughout was lack of communication between Nick and I, and a lack of counselling which created a lack of understanding.

Mental illness is the black hole of medicine. Bi polar is found in 1% of adults aged 18 and up in any given year. There are two types of bi polar disorder, bi polar I is the worst consisting of depression, mania, highs and lows, and often psychosis. Bi polar II is severe depression. Nick was bi polar I. Bi polar causes a person to self-destruct. There are no set standards of medications, tests for diagnoses, or standard procedures for treatment. A lot of it is guess work and trial and error. It can take years to find the right 'cocktail' of meds for stabilizing a patient. Talk therapy is a huge part of the treatment as well. Talk therapy should be a one on one but also include counselling for both partners in a relationship or for family members that are involved. Nick spent months taking a drug that made him crazy that together we might have been able to get changed.

The side effects of these drugs should be made known to not only the patient but to the partner or people that are affected by these things. If we had been told together about the side effects of Resperidone as in growing the 'man tits', weight gain, loss of libido, it would be something we would have worked out as a couple as it happened or be prepared when it did happen. The side effects and changes that the Abilify made in him are things we should also have been discussing together with either a doctor or counsellor on a regular basis before it got months out of hand. It was dangerous to Nick and to others. Nick didn't need his brain destroyed by that drug. He should have been taken off it a few weeks after he started not have it doubled months later.

If a drug that is supposed to change the chemical imbalance of the brain does it in a negative way how does the patient explain the changes? The partner or family member sees the changes, hears the changes and can explain what is happening. This should be part of the standard treatment.

If I wanted to know about a side effect of a drug I had to look it up on the internet. That is all good and fine but the patient and the partner need to be advised together. I could see changes in Nick and side effects that were listed such as shuffling feet, runny nose, slurring words, skin rashes but if I brought that up Nick would get angry. I don't blame him. He felt humiliated. The fact that on Abilify he lost all motivation and concentration, didn't want to read or do much was a definite sign it wasn't working properly. If that had been addressed at the beginning changes would have been made and months of hell would have been averted.

Mental illness affects the relationship and the family. Every time you read about bi polar, the opening line is that it destroys relationships. One of the things about bi polar is the absence of a conscience. A conscience changes actions. In a relationship, the job of each partner is to make the other happy. If one of the couple has lost the ability to do that, both get hurt. Finding a positive solution through counselling and working towards preventing it would save so much heartache. A person with bi polar doesn't need to be alone or running away or struggling through life with different jobs or partners. He or she deserves a good life just like the rest of us. That comes with love, understanding and forgiveness. Talking with a professional together as a couple or family or both, about the meds, moods, the difficulties of understanding the other's feelings, of Walking a Mile in My Shoes.

The person with the mental illness also needs to understand the difficulty of the life of the partner/family member. Not every day can this happen, sometimes the moods are past normal reasoning. But when the mood has passed, then the time comes for both to talk with a mediator about what happened and the resulting feelings.

There are times that the partner will be so exasperated with it all and lash out, saying things they don't mean. The partner knows the illness was responsible but still hurts from what happened during the mood and the guilt of losing their own temper. This is also hard on the person that has the bi polar.

How to handle the depression moods is a tough one. Everyone has a theory but which one actually works. This is something I handled very badly. Before Nick was diagnosed, when he spent days and nights in his chair, it would scare me, offend me, hurt me and by the time it had happened over and over I forgot how miserable he must also be for this to happen. I was angry at me because I wasn't good enough for him to come out of his moods and I didn't understand why I couldn't make him see this or that he had so much to live for. That is the illness, the person has lost reality. Depression is a place where nobody wants to be.

My therapist explained how I had made a lot of mistakes. I regret this every minute of every day. I loved this man and know I have hurt him. Yes, he made many mistakes too and also has hurt me terribly, but I understand the illness caused us both to do and say things that shouldn't have been. It doesn't even make sense the things that have happened but that is why it is called a mental illness, it is a disease of the brain. The brain doesn't operate on a normal level which is what the rest of us work on. And the rest of us begin to behave irrationally too.

A good counsellor or therapist is worth their weight in gold, but he or she has to be able to communicate with their clients and that might take time to find the right person that works this way.

It is worth the time and effort taken to find the right professional. Don't just settle.

I needed to walk in Nick's shoes through these times, and he in mine and have it explained together, talk it out together with a good mediator who knew how to keep us closer not push us further apart.

One of the nights of Nick's course was Meds night. He was really distraught after that night. Meds night should include the partners or be a separate course altogether or have a time set apart by a doctor or counsellor to address these issues before they get out of hand. The meds make physical and mental changes. All the people involved have to be ready in case these changes happen, understand the changes, give moral support and help make the information available of the negative and positive changes that occur.

The bi polar stats are scary for someone reading them. Broken into quarters they read as - suicide, surviving alone, living alone, or making it. You can hate the statistics, not the statistician, or work to change them. Pain is part of loving, hurt is part of loving, and when statistics say 75% will have pain and hurt the odds of happiness are lousy. So we work at changing those odds. Being responsible is hard work but it has its rewards. The rewards are worth being responsible.

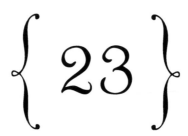

{ 23 }

FAMILY IS A HUGE PART OF THE EQUATION. FAMILY AND FRIENDS cannot take sides, make judgments such as 'you are better off without...' 'You don't deserve that kind of treatment'... and so on. In my case, I didn't have family I had friends, and he had the family. My friends wanted me to be happy and I understand that, his family needed someone to blame for his illness instead of accepting it for what it was. I don't know if his mother condoned the way Nick treated me, maybe she did. She phoned many times and the things she would say to me were horrible and it was more than I should have had to handle.

There should be no blame in mental illness. What does it accomplish? We hear about high profile cases concerning people with bi polar, those that make the six o'clock news, but hundreds of everyday people go through their life hiding or fighting this disorder alone.

When family gets older, we take care of them, when they get sick we nurture them, when a mental illness strikes, we hide it. Not all of us but a lot of the time it happens. People deserve the same love and the same compassion but it can't all be left to one person. We need to work together. There should be no stigma associated with mental illness. It is just an illness of the brain. We have not evolved from hiding lepers in colonies on an island or isolating the mentally ill in buildings with barred windows if we put labels on people.

However, the most important point of help for bi polar – any mental illness for that fact – is that the person that has the illness has to accept it and take responsibility for managing it. It cannot be cured, it is chronic. But it can be controlled. Nick didn't work at either managing or controlling it. He allowed himself to hurt me for years, emotionally, verbally, and physically. He never felt bad for any of the things he did nor said to me. He blamed me and everything in his life for his problems. When he finally hit rock bottom and decided it was time to end his life, he was given a chance to become healthy again and responsible for his future. This was when he needed to change and take an interest in how his illness was managed. It was his call to tell the professionals in his life how the meds work, how he felt, learn about the 'triggers' for different moods, and USE them. It was also his call to trust me and include me in how he was feeling so that I could help him get the right meds not the wrong ones and to understand how he was feeling. Treating me as the enemy was wrong. It was up to Nick as well to have had the correct med changes made at the time they needed to be done. He could have been seeing a psychiatrist in the city twice a month or more if he wanted to. He could have been going to groups' right from the start. All of these things were positive ways to be the best he could be and managing his illness would have done this. I tried my best to find what he needed but usually ended up butting my head against a brick wall. He had to try too.

I don't know if an earlier diagnosis would have made a difference to his illness. Thank goodness he didn't pull the trigger or yes, then it obviously would have. But from a selfish point of view, early treatment certainly would have made a difference in my life. I feel abandoned, which I am. Eight years ago, it was Nick's idea to move here and he was full of wonderful plans for improvements and making a great life together. Instead of doing things that needed doing, those that would make our life better, he started other things. Instead of moving out here and getting a job, he tried having a few animals to farm with. He was an honors student in business, he had to have known that was an impossible idea. I have finished or cleaned up his great ideas over the years, they always lost momentum after the initial excitement was over. I fixed his messes and smoothed over the problems they caused. I let myself get caught up in his illness. His illness became my life and it ruined my health, it hurt me to the core, I lost my respect for me, for who I was and am, and I have a long journey back to being a whole person again. The mess that he has left me in does not make an impression on him or maybe that is his illness or am I making excuses for him again. He stopped having any respect for me or maybe he never did, I don't know. Every woman deserves respect from the man she is with or any man for that matter. It seems he can make the choices he wants to that benefit him because he spent time lining up a place, a job and a car before he left. It was in no way a self-sacrifice. It was carefully thought out and planned. It just didn't include any responsibilities from his old life that might spoil his new one.

And there I was making this great homecoming for him, again. When I found out he had left, I was devastated. I felt ridiculous and worthless. I cried lots, I hated myself, my life, and the last eight years were a waste. What a waste of me. But with the help of wonderful friends and even strangers I have picked myself up and day by day I become stronger and even catch myself smiling now and again.

Part of the nature of the full blown bipolar person is that life is only about them and for them. Empathy for others is virtually nonexistent. I have read that it is a survival instinct the illness causes. If that is true then what is the survival mode for the bi polar person's partner? Many have told me it is to leave them. I couldn't do that, I loved him.

I often wonder if Nick was always bi polar. His step dad asked me several times if I thought he was moody. He didn't seem to be when I first met him, but I have read that self-medication such as alcohol or drugs can control moods to a certain degree. Nick was taking oxytocin for the pain in his leg, his doctor told me this could have suppressed early symptoms.

I also wonder if Nick has any idea how many times in the last few years I would have liked to run away from the life I lived with him. He went places, on trips, I stayed and looked after the farm, I worked and looked after him and in the end what was it for?

when men cross the line between what they know is right and wrong, such as the way they treat or abuse a woman, lying, cheating, drinking or gambling, the first time is the ice breaker, after that it just gets easier each time until they feel it is their right to live that way. Consequences become unjustified punishment for something that has become the normal way of living their life and they believe that it is truly how they should live.

I have packed nine years into just a few pages – there is so much more – but that would be repetitive and redundant. The important facts are here. Bi polar is livable if both people in the relationship take responsibility for managing the illness.

After reading this book, some will think Nick was an ass amongst other things, but I think I know the person inside, the person that was trapped by an illness, or, then again, maybe I don't. I thought I knew the man that used to love everything, the smart and funny guy who could make me laugh, could build anything, handle any new job and do it well, those sparkling blue eyes and wonderful smile. He had to be the best at everything because if not it wasn't acceptable for him. That was a part of his personality that some would find annoying but that was him. We all have our vices and that wasn't such a bad one.

Some will think I am a doormat, I let myself be treated badly and that I deserved it because I allowed it to continue. When you love someone the way I loved Nick, and the continual failure to help him, it made my brain ill too. I stopped doing the rational and took the abuse he handed out. I just wanted him well and upsetting him made more problems.

Walk a mile in our shoes because until you have it is impossible to make judgments. It is easy to look in from the outside and say 'well how stupid, she should have left him', or 'he wasn't that sick he didn't know what he was doing'. Both of those statements are likely correct. But hindsight is always twenty-twenty and great ideas come with experience. Lots of clichés can apply.

Yes, he has gone. He has left with nothing as he chose to do. He also made sure he had a good life to go to first. He doesn't have anything to remind him of what was important to him or what he loved which make the memories of the last nine years of his life. Maybe that is a good thing for him, maybe that is how you can leave everything behind, but I don't think so. Memories are what makes us who we are and who we become in the future. I would like to think that Nick will keep a place for me somewhere in his heart forever.

Is this a great ending to a botched up medical mess that went on for years? No, and it isn't enough to say no system is perfect and people unfortunately slip through the cracks now and again. How many times is now and again before it is too many? I can't guarantee things would have turned out differently but I know that if his illness had been diagnosed earlier and the treatments regulated properly he wouldn't have had to have his brain so tortured and his reputation questioned. If only someone had just really listened and went one step further than they did. We do our best to do things right. Mental illness is a part of our world just as any other illness, and all the people involved deserve the same rights, the same love and respect and the same expectations as any other affliction receives.

And if by chance one day, I met a man who told me he was bi polar, no I wouldn't run a mile. I would ask that he walk a mile in my shoes and ask me to walk a mile in his and then we would travel the journey together.